WRITE *to* PUBLISH

WRITE *to* PUBLISH

Writing feature articles for magazines, newspapers, and corporate and community publications

Vin Maskell & Gina Perry

ALLEN&UNWIN

Copyright © Vin Maskell & Gina Perry 1999

All rights reserved. No part of this book may be reproduced or transmitted in any form or by any means, electronic or mechanical, including photocopying, recording or by any information storage and retrieval system, without prior permission in writing from the publisher. *The Australian Copyright Act* 1968 (the Act) allows a maximum of one chapter or 10% of this book, whichever is the greater, to be photocopied by any educational institution for its educational purposes provided that the educational institution (or body that administers it) has given a remuneration notice to Copyright Agency Limited (CAL) under the Act.

First published in 1999
Allen & Unwin
83 Alexander Street
Crows Nest NSW 2065
Australia
Phone: (61 2) 8425 0100
Fax: (61 2) 9906 2218
Email: info@allenandunwin.com
Web: www.allenandunwin.com

National Library of Australia
Cataloguing-in-Publication entry:

Maskell, Vin, 1959– .
  Write to publish: writing feature articles for magazines, newspapers, and corporate and community publications.

  Includes index.
  ISBN 1 86448 998 7.

  1. Journalism—Authorship. 2. Creative writing. I. Perry, Gina. II. Title.

070.4

Set in 11/13 pt Adobe Garamond by DOCUPRO, Sydney
Printed by Australian Print Group, Maryborough, Vic.

10 9 8 7 6 5 4 3 2

To my brother Mark, for his words; to my mother Margaret, for her love. (VM)

To my parents, Pat and George, for their love and encouragement. (GP)

Contents

Preface   *xiii*

1 Writing feature articles   1
Magazines   1
Newspapers   2
Periodicals and corporate publications   2
Opportunities for writers   3
Writing styles   3
Defining feature articles   4
Purpose and technique   6
Features and fiction   6
The feature writer   6
Summary   11
Exercises   11

2 Being a professional writer   16
Physical space   16
The tools of the trade   17
Two desks   18
Your health   18
Cutting costs   19
Make time and set goals   19
Meeting deadlines   21
Don't give up your day job—yet   22

Allow time for running a business	23
Professional development and reviewing goals	23
Defamation, copyright and ethics	25
Summary	29
Exercises	30

3 Studying the marketplace — 33

The editor's baby	33
The search begins	34
Directories	35
The inside information	36
Further afield	36
Publication profiles—know your market intimately	39
Summary	40
Exercises	41

4 Good ideas — 42

Start with what you know	43
Move on to who you know	43
Study your market	44
Know your readers	44
Put your ideas antennae up	44
Write your ideas down	45
Treat ideas kindly	45
Don't talk your idea away	45
Prime your unconscious mind	45
Try something new	46
Look actively for other sources of story ideas	46
Select which ideas to write about	48
Congratulate yourself when someone beats you to it	49
Summary	51
Exercises	52

5 Types of articles — 54
Profiles — 55
Travel profiles — 56
As-told-to stories — 56
Instructional articles — 57
List articles — 58
News feature stories — 59
Promotional articles — 59
First-person articles — 59
Comment pieces — 60
Reviews — 60
Summary — 62
Exercises — 62

6 Research — 64
Your angle dictates your research — 66
Types of research — 67
Sources for research — 68
Research rules — 69
Research leads to more story ideas — 71
Summary — 73
Exercises — 74

7 Interviewing — 77
Background briefing — 77
Arranging questions — 78
Making the appointment — 78
Where to interview — 80
Dress and appearance — 81
Punctuality — 82
Those first few minutes — 82
The interview proper — 82
Dumb questions, not stupid questions — 83
Taking notes — 83
Thinking on three levels — 83
Pauses, silences and interruptions — 84

Reliable equipment	84
The last few minutes	84
After the interview	84
Transcribing	86
Phone interviews	87
On-line and e-mail interviews	88
The reluctant interviewee	88
Vetting the story	89
Enjoying the interview	89
Summary	89
Exercises	90

8 Writing skills — 92

Write well	92
Keep your reader in mind	93
Be concise	94
Avoid pompous words	95
Prune empty words	96
Avoid tautologies	96
Use concrete words	96
Keep your writing lively	97
Choose strong nouns and verbs	97
Use active voice	98
Write for rhythm and meaning	100
Summary	103
Exercises	103
Answers to exercises	106

9 Drafting and crafting — 109

Write a draft	109
Write first, edit later	110
Read your research notes	110
Revisit your angle/theme	111
Structure your story	112
Choose quotes	113
Make quotes flow	114

	Show, don't tell	115
	Draft and redraft	117
	Seek feedback	118
	Set up a writers' group	119
	Summary	120
	Exercises	121
10	**The top and the tail of the story**	**124**
	The lead	125
	Titles	126
	Precedes	129
	Endings	130
	Summary	132
	Exercises	132
11	**Adding value to your story**	**134**
	Sidebars	134
	Postscripts	136
	Quizzes	136
	Photographs	137
	Series	138
	Summary	138
	Exercises	139
12	**Presenting and selling your work**	**141**
	Query letters	141
	A successful query letter	144
	Following up the query letter	146
	Changing focus midstream	147
	Presenting query letters and articles	149
	Rejections	150
	Regular work	151
	Selling a story more than once	151
	Negotiating payment	152
	Summary	152
	Exercises	153

13 You are a published writer	154
The importance of subediting	155
The next story, and the next, and the next . . .	156
Summary	157
Exercises	157
Appendix 1 Selected articles	**158**
'McGrath's guitars' by Paul Daffey	158
'Paying the bills with artistry' by Rob Doole	161
'How to stop putting it off' by Gina Perry	164
'Putting it off' by Gina Perry	166
'Georgiana's passion' by Mary Ryllis Clark	171
'Women in racing' by Gina Perry	175
'Prejudice ruins a dream' by Gina Perry	178
'Under the sun in Kelly country' by Vin Maskell	180
'Dog days' by Barry Garner	183
'Bourke to Collins: tales of the city' by Deborah Forster	186
Appendix 2 Legal and ethical issues	**189**
Defamation and defence of defamation	189
Copyright	192
The AJA code of ethics	194
Index	*197*

Preface

When we embarked on our respective careers as freelance writers we knew how to research and we knew how to write. But nothing really prepared us for the experience of life in the marketplace—approaching editors, being rejected, getting published and finally being paid.

As teachers, each year we looked for the book that would provide our students with a good overview of writing feature articles for a range of publications. We wanted a book that was pitched at people like us, with a keen interest in writing and a desire to break into the industry.

We wanted to read interviews with people who write, buy and publish feature articles. We wanted a book that distilled everything that the beginning writer of feature articles needs to know. Here it is.

Acknowledgements

We would like to thank the following people who helped us directly and indirectly in the process of writing this book.

A special thanks to all our interviewees: Kate Arnold, Steve Bright, Jim Buckell, Mary Ryllis Clark, Maree Curtis, Michelle Griffin, Janet Hawley, Pat Hayes, Dr Kimberley

Ivory, Thornton McCamish, Brian Nankervis, Mark Pearson, Merran White and Rhonda Whitton for giving their time and sharing their experiences. Thanks to students and ex-students Yvonne Blake, Barry Garner and Rob Doole, who kindly allowed us to use their work; and to the many students who helped us sharpen our thinking and tested many of the exercises in this book.

Thanks to Kathryn Otte for her efficiency and patience with the permissions process; Derrick Moors for help with the title, and colleagues Sherryl Clark and Pia Herbert for casting an experienced eye over parts of the manuscript.

Thanks to the editors over the years who have encouraged and published us, particularly Pat Hayes and Maree Curtis for their guidance and their ability to bring out the best in us.

Thanks also to John Powers and Gerald Murnane who started it all. Thanks to Ilana Rose, Megan Fell, Kevin Walsh, everyone at Williamstown Community and Education Centre, and our colleagues at Victoria University.

Finally, a big thank you to Elizabeth Weiss and Colette Vella at Allen & Unwin, for their vision and astute feedback and to our families for their patience and support.

We are indebted to the copyright holders of the following material for giving us permission to reprint their work in this book:

ABC Legal Department, 1997, *ABC All-Media Law Handbook*, 3rd edn, ABC Books, Sydney, p. 3

Australian Copyright Council, 1998, Information Sheet no. 34, *Using Quotes and Extracts*, Australian Copyright Council, Sydney © Australian Copyright Council 1998. Reproduced with permission of the Australian Copyright Council

Australian Copyright Council, 1998, Information Sheet G13, *Writers and Copyright*, Australian Copyright Council, Sydney, © Australian Copyright Council 1998, reproduced with permission of the Australian Copyright Council

Australian Journalists' Association Section of the Media Entertainment and Arts Alliance, 1998, 'New 12 point code of ethics endorsed by members', *The Alliance Media Magazine, Winter issue*, p. 5

Clark, Mary Ryllis, 1996, 'Georgiana's Passion', *Age*, 18 May, p. 32

Daffey, Paul, 1997, 'McGrath's Guitars', *Rhythms*, no. 62, September, p. 38

Doole, Rob, 1997, 'Paying the bills with artistry', unpublished

Flanagan, Martin, 1994, 'The stories that must be told', *Age Student Update*, 18 April, p. 3

Forster, Deborah, 1997, 'Bourke to Collins: tales of the city', 11 April, *Age*, *Metro* supplement, p. 1

Garner, Barry, 1997, 'Dog days', 29 September, *Age*, *Metro* supplement, p. 1

Haddock, Kate, 1998, *Copyright Speech, The Future of Freelancing: Selected Papers*, Australian Journalists' Association Section of the Media, Entertainment and Arts Alliance

Kiely, Michael, 1992, 'From Oz to Oz biz', *Marketing*, July, p. 10

Pearson, Mark, 1997, *The Journalist's Guide to Media Law*, Allen & Unwin, Sydney, p. 113

The Big Issue Australia, 1998, Guidelines for contributors

Victoria University of Technology Editorial Committee, 1998, 'And it's gold, gold, gold to Australia', *Learn for Your Life*, VUT, Melbourne p. 52

White, Sally A., 1996, *Reporting in Australia*, 2nd edn, Macmillan, Melbourne, p. 95

one Writing feature articles

The reward in non-fiction writing is that the investigation is endless. There is always another house to visit, another street to walk down, another person's story to hear. Non-fiction writing is about being open to the infinite variety of the world in which we live and the essential strangeness of human experience.

Martin Flanagan, writer, *Age*, 18 April 1994

Australians are big readers of newspapers and big buyers of magazines. In the past twenty years, the number of magazines published in this country has grown dramatically, and newspapers themselves have grown in size.

Magazines

According to Roy Morgan Research, more Australians are reading magazines than newspapers. We spent nearly $800 million on magazines in 1997–1998. And it's not just the people who buy the magazines that read them. Circulation figures record copies sold, not copies read. According to A. Ring, readers have been estimated at three and ten times the circulation figures. This means some popular magazines with circulations of around one million can reach between three and ten million people (A. Ring, 1997, 'Keeping the sexist flame alive—why do magazines keep doing it?', *Australian Studies in Journalism*, no. 6, pp. 3–40).

Newspapers

While the number of newspapers in Australia has declined in the past twenty years, the total number of newspaper pages published has grown. According to the Newspaper Advertising Bureau of Australia (NABA), in 1986, 76 billion newspaper pages were published. By 1997 this had risen to 104 billion. Between 1986 and 1997 the number of pages published annually grew by 37 per cent.

Newspapers are thicker, and offer their readers more information than they ever have before. While news content has fallen slightly, according to the NABA, the number of pages covering sport and lifestyle, entertainment and consumer information has increased.

There are more supplements and weekend magazines in newspapers now than there were ten years ago with Sunday pages up 60 per cent since 1991. In fact, weekend magazines are a relatively new addition to newspapers—*The Sydney Morning Herald*'s *Good Weekend* began in 1984 and the *Australian Magazine* began in 1988.

Periodicals and corporate publications

Newsletters, journals and corporate publications have also mushroomed. *Margaret Gee's Australian Media Guide*, which is published quarterly, lists all Australian media outlets, state by state. The 2000 media outlets listed in 1987 included newspapers, magazines, newsletters, journals and trade magazines as well as radio and television. By 1998 the listing had grown to 3500 outlets. This growth in the number, size and range of publications means there has also been a growth in demand for material to fill them.

Opportunities for writers

Between the covers of each magazine, newspaper, or periodical you read you'll find a range of writing by a range of people.

Staff writers are those people employed on a salary to write for that publication. Even if what they've written isn't published, the writer on staff will still be paid. In newspapers and larger magazines, these people are usually trained journalists.

Regular contributors are people, not necessarily trained as journalists, who are paid to write a regular column or section. The contributor may be an expert in their field, a 'personality', or a writer with a particularly quirky or interesting way of writing about the world.

Freelance contributors offer their stories or ideas for stories to a publication and are usually paid by the word for stories that are published. Freelancers can write for a number of publications and can be commissioned to write stories by an editor, but they are not on staff. Freelancers can be trained journalists, or they may have gained experience via publication, serving their 'apprenticeship' long enough to have established a reputation for themselves.

These categories are fluid—staff writers may leave their employment to take up freelancing, or secure a niche as a regular contributor with one or more publications. Writers who start as freelancers can move on to regular contributing and may even be employed on staff.

Writing styles

Open any magazine, journal or newspaper that's lying around at home and you'll see there are a range of writing styles inside. In a large metropolitan daily newspaper, there are hard and soft news stories, editorial, opinion or comment pages, letters to the editor, how-to articles, and information on weather and TV viewing. Within specific supplements—employment, food and wine, cars, business, entertainment, home living, travel—you'll find reviews, feature articles, news snippets and so on.

Turn to a magazine and you'll find departments devoted to anything from fashion and beauty to food and health, home ideas and puzzles, with features often in a department all of their own.

Corporate, community and government periodicals can contain stories on new services, changes in policies, news and gossip.

Many people think of writing for newspapers when they think of writing feature articles. But the well-written factual story has its place in a host of publications: inflight magazines, corporate newsletters, publications put out by your local council or your union, to name a few.

You'll find feature articles in professional journals, magazines aimed at people in particular trades or industries, newsletters for corporate or community groups, niche or popular magazines and newspapers—local, regional, daily and weekly.

Defining feature articles

The best way to define a feature article is to think of it on a continuum with the traditional hard news story at one end and the feature at the other. Hard news includes stories that have either just happened or are about to happen, such as bushfires, crimes, court cases, protest meetings or tax reforms. The hard news story is an account of what happened, why it happened, when and where it happened, who was involved and how readers will be affected.

Take, for example, a hard news story about changes to Austudy. At a minimum, the hard news story would tell us what the proposed changes are, when, where and by whom the announcement was made, and how students will be affected by the changes.

The hard news story can be brief, and answers the key questions concisely. It is written objectively. The traditional news story has a particular shape called the inverted pyramid because the most important facts are at the top.

At the other end of the the continuum, the shape and structure of a feature article can vary enormously, from pure entertainment to serious information and every combination in between. Its length can be anything from 300–3000 words, sometimes longer.

Features differ from hard news stories in that they explore the news in more depth and focus on the human element. Let's look at the Austudy story again as an example. Who are the people most affected by the changes announced? Students, naturally. Oh, and their parents. And possibly university staff. Let's take students. They will have less money as a result.

One feature might look at three students at different institutions, how much they live on now and how the changes will affect them. Another feature might be an anecdotal piece about getting by on a pittance as a student. A third article could be a list article on the top ten opportunity shops for students looking for quality second-hand clothing. Another feature may explore the developments and changes in government policy towards financial support for students over the years.

Other types of features include those that look at changes in our lifestyles, how-to stories, self-help articles and first-person stories. Feature articles explore an issue in more depth than a hard news story.

Feature articles are not essays containing your views on

topics such as capital punishment, abortion or anything else. Yes, these opinions often do turn up in magazines and newspapers but they are clearly under a heading such as 'editorial' or 'opinion'.

Purpose and technique

The purpose of a feature article is to inform and engage the reader. Feature articles can make you laugh or cry, feel enraged or elated. The feature writer has much more scope than the writer of the traditional hard news story. Techniques for feature writing include description, narration and dramatic storytelling.

Feature stories hone in on the human element of a story, giving readers the sense that they are there alongside the writer. This demands different techniques of the writer than the hard news story.

Features and fiction

Feature writing can be as creative, demanding and enjoyable as writing short fiction or poetry. The best features are as engaging and interesting as good short stories. While factual, they use many of the same techniques as fiction writing. They expand the reader's view of the world in some way, and they are absorbing and satisfying to read.

Whether you want to write for a community group, a magazine, a corporate publication or a newspaper, you are writing because you want to tell a story. Good feature articles have all the factual detail of hard news stories, and all the drama, action and dialogue of a good short story.

The feature writer

You need to write well to be a published feature writer, but that's only part of the equation. You also need perseverance, a nose for a good story, a dedication to meeting deadlines and a passion for accuracy. Throw in creativity and curiosity, and you've got all the ingredients required. Last but not least, you need to be an addicted reader of everything—newsletters, magazines, newspapers, anything that comes your way.

Have a nose for a good story

Having a nose for a good story means developing an instinct for what your readers will be interested in, which is critical as a feature writer. Before you start writing you have to have a clear idea of who your reader is, and so you need to study the publication you want to write for. You'll see more on this in chapters 3 and 4.

Be an avid reader

The best advice we have for you as a feature writer is to read, read, read. And of course, write, write, write. By doing this you will absorb many of the rules that govern this form, you'll expose yourself to a range of different styles and, best of all, you'll be full of new ideas that have come from what you've read.

As a newspaper and magazine junkie you'll pick up lots of tips on writing features by reading them. You'll learn about the different forms they take—travel, self-help, profile, interview, lifestyle pieces—as well as elements such as sidebars, quizzes, postscripts and photographs, which add value to a feature. You'll read more about this in chapters 5 and 11. See sample articles in appendix 1.

Appreciate the importance of accuracy and the pursuit of facts

Feature articles originated and evolved in newspapers. They were and are written by journalists, who have training in reporting news. You'll need to be able to listen and observe carefully, and present details and opinions accurately and objectively. Your opinion is not the stuff of features. Opinions in a feature are most likely to be attributed to someone you interviewed for the story. You'll see more on this in chapter 6.

Enjoy research

You need to enjoy finding things out, tracking information down, interviewing people to get the story. Be curious about people and events and get excited about conveying what you know to your reader. You'll see more on this in chapters 6 and 7.

Combine love of language with an economic writing style

We assume you have a love of language and a solid grasp of grammar. As for an economic writing style, brevity and clarity are the key words here. Using as few words as possible to get your meaning across is an essential skill for writing features. Look more closely at exercises to develop this in chapter 8.

Make a piece of writing come alive and flow

As well as being able to write clearly and concisely, you need to be able to structure a piece of writing in a logical way. You also need to know how to hook your reader with your lead, and how to make them feel satisfied by your ending. See chapters 9 and 10.

Persevere

You may be good enough to get your first feature published quickly, but rejection is inevitable. Get used to it. Developing a thick skin when it comes to rejection is important because it helps you put some distance between yourself and your work.

Many beginning writers take rejection personally, confusing rejection of their story with rejection of themselves as people. Remember, a story can be sent back because there is simply not enough space in the publication, not enough dollars in the budget or it wasn't right for the publication.

Don't expect detailed feedback from editors on your work. They are too busy for one thing, and it's not their job. If you want an opinion on your work, join or set up your own writing group. Learn to put your story away and come back to it with a fresh eye and a sharpened pencil, to see if you can improve anything about the story. We'll cover how to improve your story and workshopping in chapter 9. We'll cover how to add value to your story to improve its chances of publication in chapter 11.

Be guided by legal and ethical considerations

Essential for anyone interested in feature writing is knowledge of the ethics and legalities of what you are doing. See chapter 2 and appendix 2.

Be professional

Be reliable. Never miss a deadline. Study the publication you're writing for. Be accurate. Double check facts. All of these qualities will endear you to an editor and will assure that you develop a solid reputation as a writer who can be relied on. As a truly professional writer, treat feature writing the same way you would treat any small business you would like to set up and run successfully. See chapters 2, 12 and 13.

In this book we will give you tips on how to start, how to shape a piece of writing, how to make it easy to read and interesting to your reader. All the exercises in this book are aimed at helping you find your own particular style.

On completing her cadetship with the Sun News-Pictorial, *Maree Curtis specialised in medical reporting. She has worked as Melbourne editor of* Woman's Day, *was founding editor of* Mind and Body, *the* Herald-Sun's *health section, and editor of* The Sunday Age's Life! *section. She is currently a senior features writer on the* Age.

As an editor, what I look for in a feature article is relevance. There are a million topics in the world and I'll ask myself when I'm looking at a feature, Why am I looking at this story today?

In newspapers features are always dealing with something coming off the back of news. Even if the news values are not obvious, with something like a celebrity profile for example, the story will be linked to a new book, a film or something the celebrity has said or done.

An editor also needs to have established that the freelancer is trustworthy and accurate. It is really important for editors to be able to trust that the freelancer has done the interview they've said they've done, that the case studies they've used are real, that they have reported accurately and fairly and in a balanced way. This is second nature to a trained journalist but not necessarily to a freelancer. You might write like an angel but your copy is useless unless it is relevant, accurate, balanced and checked.

The ideal freelancer is someone who can spin a yarn, tell a story. You have to be able to engage and involve people in the story you're telling. You need to be brief. Telling an interesting story about a person in 800 words is a real skill.

Be a 'can do' person. Sit up all night if you have to to meet your deadline. You can sleep the next day. Say yes if you can deliver. Never, ever let an editor down unless you're in hospital with a broken neck and even then you can still type! Editors are only interested in people who can deliver on time copy that is useable.

Read, read, read—read to find a style you admire, read to find stuff you don't admire. Analyse stories that don't work for you and try and work out why they don't work. Of course, you've got to love language to be able to write.

You have to be everything a journo is plus. What have you got that a journo hasn't? Expertise. You don't have to have high-powered training. It might be a hobby. Your hobby might be toy trains and no one else is covering it. You might be able to carve a niche and be an expert.

If you want to express your opinion, aim for the opinion pages. In features no one is interested in what you think. You are a conduit between the people with the information and your readers. Your opinion is irrelevant. Keep it out of the story.

Summary

Feature writers:

- have a nose for a good story and a strong sense of curiosity
- are avid readers
- enjoy research
- appreciate the importance of accuracy and the pursuit of facts
- combine love of language with an economic writing style
- can make their writing come alive and flow
- persevere
- are guided by ethical and legal frameworks
- are professional

Exercises

1. Make a list of all the newspapers, magazines and periodicals that you read (even half read) in an average week.

2. Metropolitan daily papers are divided up into different sections or supplements. There are different supplements every day. Look at your daily paper over a seven-day period. Make a list of each day's supplements and the names of the editors responsible for them.

3. Estimate how much space in your daily paper is given to the following:
   - news—Australian, overseas
   - sport
   - service information—weather, TV guide, classified ads
   - advertising
   - editorial, opinion pieces, regular columns, reviews
   - feature articles

4. Find a hard news story in your newspaper. Now find a feature article on the same subject. Compare the two. List the differences you can see between them.

5. Look at four or five issues of your favourite magazine. Make a list of the regular departments or sections and make a list of the kinds of writing you can find over the issues—news, how-to, profiles, interviews, opinion pieces, editorial and so on.

6. Collect six or seven different periodicals put out by government or community agencies—newsletters, journals and so on. Analyse them the way you have done with your newspaper and favourite magazines.

7. Read the Richard Walsh excerpt that follows. What did your parents/uncles/aunts/grandparents read when you were a child? How has this influenced your reading habits?

8. Talk to a freelance writer who writes for magazines, newspapers or the corporate sector about how they started and what they see as the essential requirements of feature writing.

From Oz to Oz biz by Michael Kiely

Richard Walsh, former 'ratbag journalist' and fringe publisher, has his hands on the reins of this country's largest periodical group as it rides the wild horses of popular taste. Michael Kiely reports.

Richard Walsh has come a long way in the last three decades. From the obscenity of *Oz* magazine to the pinstripes of *Australian Business*. From the left-leaning *Nation Review* to the crudely macho, 'girl in dog collar' style of *People* magazine.

While never a bomb-thrower on the barricades, Richard Walsh played an active role in the student revolt against the post-Menzies establishment. He is now managing director of Australian Consolidated Press, the behemoth of Australian magazine publishing.

The transition should not be surprising. In the '70s, many US corporations hired former student radicals because they had the skills required for success in business. They could lead a rabble. They could articulate and create a sense of common purpose.

Mr Walsh is such a leader. A former industrial psychologist and medical graduate—he wanted to become a psychiatrist—he now uses his feel for the mass mind to move magazines in their millions off newsagency shelves.

In his time as publisher, ACP has grown from $74m to $112.25m in profit before tax between 1989 and 1991. It was recently floated on the stock exchange and valued at $1.175 billion. (Mr Walsh was the public face of the float, taking the message to the markets via presentations around the country.)

The ACP phenomenon reveals important characteristics of the Australian consumer.

We are a magazine-mad race. Every Australian buys on average 27 magazines each year. The three leading women's magazines sell in excess of a million copies per issue.

We have more titles per head of population than any other nation on earth. The Australian network of newsagencies—which are in effect supermarkets for magazines—is the envy of the rest of the world. While we take it for granted, there are many countries where most households do not contain magazines.

'One of the reasons why Australia is such a great magazine country is that *Women's Weekly*—and later *New Idea* and *Woman's Day*—has been so successful,' says Richard Walsh. 'Most people are raised in households where the mother reads magazines. Children from a very early age see magazine reading as an everyday pastime.'

Australia has a tradition of magazine reading that goes back beyond the *Women's Weekly* to the days before Federation when shearers in the back blocks would eagerly wait for the mail to bring *The Bulletin* ('the bushman's bible') and *The Lone Hand*, fiercely nationalistic, republican, and racist magazines which carried the works of Banjo Patterson, Henry Lawson, and C. J. Dennis.

They were the first to speak with an independent Australian voice and played a unifying role during the process which led to the birth of the Commonwealth. 'They were the start of so-called Australian culture because they were prepared to write about the Australian experience,' says Mr Walsh.

And they laid the foundation for the male tradition of magazine reading among the masses. 'While in some countries magazine reading is a woman's activity, there is a long tradition in Australia of men reading magazines, which continues today, even among young men,' he says, pointing to the large circulations of titles like *Street Machine*, *Rugby League Week*, and the 'barber-shop magazines' *Australasian Post*, *People* and *Picture*.

'Young girls also move into reading magazines at an early age, earlier than in other countries,' he says. Titles such as *Dolly* and *Girlfriend* attract large followings.

Australian magazine readers have 3000 to choose from, 500 of them home-grown. While Mr Walsh believes they contribute to the 'mad soup of opinion around the place', they can also create a major headache for media buyers and advertisers.

'In our lifetime, no one is going to start a big metro

newspaper, nor will there be new broadcast TV channels. But literally every week, possibly every day, a new magazine starts up. It is an endless process,' he says.

'I liken it to a rainforest: big timber comes down, new trees come up. It's a microcosm of life.' . . .

Reproduced with permission from *Marketing* magazine, July 1992.

two Being a professional writer

If you want to become a writer, I believe the most important thing is to treat your writing as a business. You need to develop expertise in writing what your readers want to know—not what you want them to read—and then produce a structured, practical piece of prose.

Rhonda Whitton, freelance writer

Without qualifications you've got to do your time. Get a start where you can—local papers, free papers, you may have to start out writing for nothing. Student newspapers are often very happy to have someone volunteering.

Merran White, freelance writer

To write feature articles you need to think and work professionally. This means setting up a work space as well as developing attitudes and habits that encourage you to be productive and professional.

Physical space

Find yourself a distinct space that is always available for you to work in. A section of a bedroom could be workable but a separate room is ideal. You will work much better if you can make phone calls without the sound of the television in the background, and if you can write and research without being interrupted by children, co-tenants, cats or dogs. You need to be away from the distractions of household life around you.

You may be able to rent cheap office space near your home. You could cut costs by sharing the room/s with somebody else. This can also help you to avoid the isolation that can come with being a writer.

The tools of the trade

You don't need every piece of state-of-the-art information technology to be a good writer. You will need some office equipment to run a good business, but there's no need to break the bank.

Personal computers seem to be getting better, and cheaper, all the time. And word processing packages make life a lot easier for those who are serious about writing and rewriting. But don't rush into buying a computer. Shop around. Check consumer guides. Ask friends and colleagues what equipment they use.

The telephone is a key research tool, while answering machines or voicemail are now standard office equipment. Access to fax, the Internet and e-mail makes your work much easier. A reliable camera is essential if you intend to include photographs with your stories.

A good filing system is a must. You don't need miles of filing cabinets—rather a system that allows you quick and ready access to information you need. Mary Ryllis Clark, freelance travel/history writer, recommends the following:

> Keeping material organised used to be a big problem before I got a room of my own. I now keep all my reference books in shelves in my office. I have three filing cabinets full of files relating to

places in Victoria, Australia and overseas but also themes, topics etc.

In addition I keep all my used A4 envelopes and when I have been on a fact finding trip, I put all the material for a specific place in one envelope. I must confess I also use the floor. When I am in the middle of a story which requires a number of references, my room looks fairly chaotic. I think I know where and what everything is—but my system is not foolproof.

Two desks

If you can afford it (and if you've got the space), consider two desks: one just for the computer and all its bits and pieces, and one for your paperwork—somewhere to jot down ideas, make phone calls, re-read drafts. It is important to separate the different tasks involved in writing. Use two desks to do this.

For all the wonders of computers, it is important to sometimes work without the hum of the machinery, to just place several pages of an article-in-progress over a desk and simply look at the story. There's nothing wrong with slowing down, with just pondering the pages and musing upon the words, the structure and the idea of the story.

Your health

Some occupational hazards of being a writer include poor posture, back pain, eye strain, and repetitive strain injury (RSI) for starters. Take time to plan your office with your own health and safety in mind. Make sure:

- your chair is comfortable and good for your posture
- the lighting in your workspace is adequate
- the keyboard is set at a comfortable angle
- the desk and chair are the right height

- cords, leads and plugs are neatly placed together, not snaking across the floor
- your power point is not overloaded

Cutting costs

You may need to be thrifty in setting up your office. Not everything has to be brand new. Try op-shops, second-hand dealers and schools for pre-loved items such as filing cabinets, bookshelves and noticeboards.

For reference books, try your luck at your local library's annual booksale. Yes, the books will be a little out of date but they can still come in handy.

Stationery is also important. Personalised stationery will enhance the professionalism of your work and desktop publishing means you can do your own letterheads. Just don't go overboard on the design.

Enjoy yourself while you're setting up your room, but don't use it as a form of procrastination. After all, a beautifully organised and spacious office with state-of-the-art equipment is useless if you don't have some good ideas in your head.

Make time and set goals

Set yourself achievable goals, and write them down. Impose homemade deadlines on your work. Eventually editors will do this for you, so you may as well get in some practice. Be ambitious with your goals, but also be realistic. Such goals will depend on your personal circumstances and levels of skill and confidence.

You could set yourself:

- a certain amount of hours per week
- a particular amount of words per week
- a specific number of ideas and query letters per month

- a definite number of completed stories per month
- a definite number of published articles per month
- a necessary amount of income per month

Steve Bright is a corporate journalist who has won a string of national awards. His clients have included Telstra, Orica and Price Waterhouse. Here he reflects on his various workplaces.

For the first three years of my professional writing life I worked from the spare bedroom in my small inner-suburban flat. I was my own master, but it didn't work. I found it was becoming increasingly difficult to 'switch off', to separate work from home and vice-versa. I worked too long, too hard, too late, always rushing to meet the deadlines of other people. In the end I found I could barely walk past that door without going in for just a few minutes, whether it was six in the morning or eleven at night. I put a lock on the door, gave my wife the key and told her to restrict me to reasonable access. Then, of course, I got angry and blamed her.

I had a few regular clients and was more or less paying the bills, so I moved into my first 'office'—a converted garage at my in-laws house. I painted it bright yellow and sat there waiting for the phone to ring. It didn't much, but at least I had somewhere I could meet with a client or interview someone.

The next big move was to a loft in a portside suburb. It felt good to go to work in the morning, then, at the end of the day, to lock the door and go home. Also, people seemed to take me more seriously if there was a name on the door and I wasn't sharing the phone with the household.

In between times I would sometimes work as a sub-contractor, writing on an hourly rate for a client, in their office. I found this quite satisfying. You meet colleagues, experience new ideas, new chat. I don't do it five days a week, but one or two is OK. You may not be your own master, but at least you do not have the responsibility of running the place at a profit.

Today I mostly work in a converted 'granny flat' on a country block. With fax, modem, e-mail, Internet and overnight courier bags, the demand for face-to-face contact is not what it once was.

Meeting deadlines

Meeting deadlines is critical for your survival as a professional writer. Plan ahead.

1. Make a note in your diary of when the job is due. Work backwards from that date and calculate how much time you've got.

2. Make a list of all the stages of the job—research, telephone calls, library visits, drafting, redrafting, the lot. Breaking a large project into bits makes it less overwhelming and it seems more achievable.

3. Allocate time to each stage. Then double it.

4. Allow time in the schedule for the unexpected disaster— the car breaking down, the computer crashing—and build it into your schedule.

5. Plan time to daydream or relax between drafts. That way you give yourself a chance to have some inspired ideas.

6. Take one task at a time and reward yourself for completing it.

7. Remember your first and early drafts don't have to be perfect. They are a means of getting your thoughts in order and working out what you want to say.

8. If, despite all this, the unexpected does occur and you

can't make the deadline, ring your editor and let them know ahead of time. That way you save your reputation and give the editor time to find something else to fill the space.

Don't give up your day job—yet

If you're hoping to make a comfortable living from writing articles, be realistic. If you've got a day job, keep it for a while longer. Unless you have an enormous workrate or a flair for marketing your work all around the world, you're not likely to be making a living out of freelancing immediately.

Start with small articles for small publications, scoring by-lines and free copies. If you are a student, get published in your student paper. If you're a worker, aim for a professional journal or workplace newsletter. It might not pay but it is a step on the road towards professional, paying publications.

Set a limit on how long you will write for free. Your work may be taken for granted and the standard of your writing may not be pushed. Don't underestimate the symbolic power of money. Not being paid for stories can feed a feeling that your writing is not up to standard.

When you are ready to submit to paying publications, check out rates of pay for the publications you intend writing for. Pay rates vary widely. The Australian Journalists' Association, a section of the Media Entertainment and Arts Alliance, provides information on rates for freelancers. Before you approach an editor with a story be aware of what your bottom line is when it comes to negotiating a price.

Be aware, too, of the different systems of payment. Some publications pay on acceptance—which means you get paid immediately even if the story is not published for several weeks or months. Others pay on publication—which means you get paid a few weeks after the article has been published. If you're working as a writer in the corporate sector you may be paid by the hour, or by the size of the job, rather than by word length.

Allow time for running a business

Allow time in your schedule for all the tasks associated with running your own business. They include making phone calls, issuing and following up invoices, keeping records, filing ideas, articles and receipts—running an office, basically.

Professional development and reviewing goals

Develop networks and join professional associations. Identify your weaknesses and work to correct them. Pursue courses or other means of updating and extending your skills.

Regularly review your goals and make time to develop your skills. This means keeping up with changes in current publications, and noticing new ones starting up.

Rhonda Whitton worked for 21 'long' years in human resources and studied for a degree majoring in journalism. While working she moonlighted as a freelance journalist and served a ten-year 'apprenticeship' before becoming a full-time freelancer. She has been published in most metropolitan newspapers including the Herald Sun, *the* Brisbane Sunday Mail, *the* Adelaide Advertiser, *the* Canberra Times *and* The West Australian *as well as numerous adventure, travel and outdoor magazines. She works as a freelancer as well as teaching and compiling* The Australian Writer's Marketplace: the Complete Guide to Being Published.

Becoming a freelance writer doesn't happen overnight. When first starting out, your primary focus should be on building up a portfolio of published works. It makes sense to begin writing as a hobby then, once your by-lines begin to appear, do your sums and calculate whether you can survive from your earnings. If possible, arrange to take time off from your job or studies to see if the hours and lonely lifestyle suits.

My work habits are very regular and I try to keep the same hours as when I worked for a boss. But if you prefer less conventional hours, then tap into your natural body rhythms and work whenever it feels right, whether that be at 4 am or 3 pm. As well, let your family know that your writing is a business. I have a room set up as an office. When I start work, I let my partner know in no uncertain terms that 'I'm going to work now'.

While it is becoming increasingly important to have modern technology like a fax, Internet access and a scanner, you would be wise to invest in those expensive tools later—after you've made a commitment to become a freelancer and begin earning money. I've always been a meticulous record keeper and that certainly helps, as does a good tax agent. Because there will be peaks and troughs in your income, you do need to have a healthy bank balance before you start—or a rich partner. As well, you need a certain strength of character and maturity to cope with tight deadlines and editors' whims.

I started by writing for my local newspaper and even though it was unpaid, seeing my by-line was the ultimate adrenalin rush. At that stage, money wasn't a consideration—adding to my portfolio was more important.

After being advised by my journalism professor that I should never give my words away for free, I went to my university library and asked to see the books telling me where I could get my work published. The librarians showed me British and American books, but there was no Australian version.

For ten years I waited for such a book to appear on the booksellers' shelves, but it didn't happen. Eventually I thought, well if no one else is going to do it, I will! I approached a publisher who agreed there was a niche in the marketplace for such a book and *The Australian Writer's Marketplace* is now published annually.

Defamation, copyright and ethics

Freelancing, and professional writing in general, requires an understanding of some legal and ethical issues. These issues affect all stages of the writing process: researching, interviewing, quoting from other material and ownership of your work.

Defamation

To defame a person is to publish material that damages someone's reputation. A writer can be sued for defamation, even if the article does not name the person who is being defamed.

There have been a handful of well-publicised defamation cases in Australia over the past two decades. These include the 1984 Leo Schofield restaurant review in *The Sydney Morning Herald*, in which the owners of a restaurant received $100 000 in damages after a particularly negative review; and the photograph in *HQ Magazine* of rugby league player Andrew Ettinghausen, which led to a $100 000 defamation payout. The photograph, taken without Ettinghausen's consent, showed him naked in a football club's change rooms.

In 1999, the ACT Supreme Court awarded more than $277 000 to the Federal Treasurer, Peter Costello, the Employment Services Minister, Tony Abott, and their wives over a passage in the Bob Ellis book, *Goodbye Jerusalem*.

Mark Pearson, associate professor of journalism at Bond University, Queensland, offers the following advice for novice writers:

> Put yourself in the shoes of the person you're writing about. Think of that person's attitudes, beliefs and principals and ask if the words being used would upset that person. Are you writing something you wouldn't like written about yourself? The old adage of 'If in doubt, leave out' is still pretty good. If you still want to go with the story, check with your editor, or the publication's legal advisers.

How does an editor view defamation? Thornton McCamish is the editor of *The Big Issue*, a magazine sold by the homeless and long-term unemployed in Melbourne, Sydney and Brisbane. He is proud that the magazine can explore controversial issues but he won't risk a defamation suit.

> We're an independent publication so we like to keep things edgy. But our primary loyalty is staying afloat, so that the vendors on the streets have got work. We won't risk losing the publication. The overall project of *The Big Issue* is more important than the words, the opinion, of a contributor who wants to say something that could be defamatory.

You must take responsibility for your own work and always consider the impact of your stories on other people. For further information on defamation, see appendix 2.

Copyright

As a writer copyright affects you in two ways: your ownership of your work, and your use of other people's work.

Copyright and ownership of your work

According to Australian Copyright Council advice:

> Works of writing—such as novels, poems and newspaper articles—are automatically protected by copyright as soon as they are written or otherwise recorded in some way (for example, on computer disk). You do not have to register your work or go through any other procedure.

Although the copyright symbol is not necessary 'it does notify people that the work is protected and identifies the person claiming the right'. You can place the symbol on your work yourself—on each page of an article if you wish, or on the first and last pages. The copyright symbol, or notice, is usually followed by the writer's name and the year of first publication: © Jill Smith 1999.

Copyright is the right to copy or publish a work. You hold the copyright on your own work unless you sell that right to someone else. As the copyright holder, you may give or sell someone permission to copy or publish your work without relinquishing your copyright entirely—this is called granting non-exclusive rights. When you sell a feature article, you should be clear whether you are handing over copyright entirely or granting non-exclusive rights over your work.

If you work as a freelancer—generating ideas for stories and approaching editors with those stories—you are the owner of the copyright of your work. If you are employed by a magazine or newspaper or corporation, your employer usually owns the copyright to material that you have written in the course of your job.

Manage your copyright with care. Read contracts and fine print carefully. Put a standard clause on work you submit that makes it clear what rights you are selling in which particular publications.

Kate Haddock, copyright expert with Banki Haddock Fiora, said the following in a speech at the Australian Journalists' Association's Future of Freelancing convention, Melbourne, 1998:

> Copyright is your property. It is important to identify what you own and then protect it . . . As a general rule, if you created a work and it is original, you own the copyright in the work. Consider the following:
>
> - Do you want your work to be included in other publications? If so, how do you want to be paid for those additional uses? Do you want to approve the use prior to publication?
> - Do you want your work to be put on the Internet? Do you want to approve its placement prior to publication? What

about CD-ROMs and databases? Is access to the database going to be paid for?
- What type of payment do you want for use? Royalty or flat free or some other structure?

Copyright is very easy to steal. It is also relatively complex and extremely valuable. Don't give it away without good reason.

If in doubt, get advice. There is a lot of free and cheap advice from various copyright advisory centres, including the Australian Copyright Council and the Arts Law Centre of Australia.

Copyright and the use of someone else's work

It would be a very dull world if we couldn't occasionally quote small extracts from other articles, from poems, songs, films and novels. The key to quoting from other sources is to acknowledge those sources. If you want your own work to be properly acknowledged, extend the professional courtesy to fellow writers.

When you intend to quote a substantial part of a work, you will need to seek permission in writing from the owners of the copyright of the material (who may or may not be the author). What is 'substantial' is not defined in the Copyright Act. Ask yourself if the part you want to quote is substantial in relation to the work as a whole. If you're not sure, it is best to seek permission. In all cases, whether you are quoting a small portion or a large one, you must attribute the original source of the material. If you don't, you are creating an impression, deliberately or otherwise, that the quoted material is your own. Then you can be accused of plagiarism.

Attributing the source of your quote does not mean interrupting the flow of the story with lengthy or technical information. Attributions should not be put in as footnotes or in a list of references as they are in essays; rather they should be woven into the text of story.

You can also occasionally paraphrase another writer's words. To paraphrase is to rewrite somebody else's material in your own words, while still retaining the sense of what the writer means. You are still required to acknowledge your sources when paraphrasing.

For example, you could paraphrase the preceding paragraph in this way:

> Vin Maskell and Gina Perry in their book, *Write to Publish*, suggest that you can occasionally paraphrase another writer. This means to rewrite another person's words without losing the meaning of those words. Maskell and Perry also emphasise that it is important to state where your material comes from.

For further information on copyright, see appendix 2.

Code of ethics

As a professional writer you have certain ethical responsibilities. The Australian Journalists' Association (AJA), is part of the Media, Entertainment and Arts Alliance (MEAA). Since 1993 the AJA has been working on a new code of ethics to replace previous versions. This proposed code offers guidelines for the behaviour and professional standards of journalists, whether they work in print, radio, television or other forms of communication. Although geared more towards reporters of hard news, the code still provides a useful framework for behavior and standards for many types of non-fiction writers.

The code promotes individual responsibility and the basic values of honesty, fairness, independence and respect for the rights of others. The code is reproduced in full in appendix 2.

Summary

- Writing feature articles is a business
- Ideally, you need a room of your own
- Plan your workspace with health and safety in mind

- Don't break the bank when setting up your office
- Develop consistent work habits
- Allow time for running a business
- Set yourself achievable goals—aim for small, even non-paying, publications at first
- Develop your skills
- Regularly review your goals
- Keep up with changes in the market
- Defamation is publishing something which harms the reputation of another person
- A person can be defamed even if they are not named in an article
- There is no formal procedure for registering copyright
- The copyright symbol is not necessary but it does notify people you own copyright
- Always attribute your sources and get permission where necessary. This should prevent you from infringing another writer's copyright
- A code of ethics describes acceptable practice and it is up to you to measure your professional conduct against the code to ensure that you report honestly, fairly and independently, and that you respect the rights of others

Exercises

1. Describe your ideal writing and work space. Limit yourself to 500 words.

2. Compare your ideal with the real. What changes need to be made to make you a more effective writer?

3. Develop a writing timetable for the next week then review it. Did you work to it? If not, why not?

4. Establish some realistic goals for your article writing. Then do a step-by-step plan for reaching those goals.

5. Devise a business plan on paper. Your plan should be based around your answers to the following questions.

    - Who will buy my material? Describe who your market is. Do some research to establish that they buy freelance material. Are your markets local, interstate, overseas?
    - Who are the other writers that you are competing against in the markets you have identified?
    - What do you have to offer that your competitors don't? Describe what is unique about you—your experience, your expertise, your niche.

6. Look at the following list of general subject areas. How many of them interest you? How many of them could you write about?

    - Health
    - Environment
    - History
    - Business
    - Relationships
    - Family life
    - Travel
    - Money
    - Psychology
    - Happiness
    - Women
    - New technology
    - Religion

7. Who, apart from the writer, can be sued for defamation? (See appendix 2.)

8. Contact the Australian Copyright Council (telephone 02 9318 1788 or website www.copyright.org.au), to

obtain the following information sheets: *Writers and Copyright*, *Newsletters and Copyright*, *Quotes and Extracts*.

9. Look at the article in appendix 1 titled 'Under the Sun in Kelly Country'. How has the writer made it clear that the lyrics he is quoting are songwriter Paul Kelly's?

10. What does the AJA code of ethics say about plagiarism? (See appendix 2.)

threeStudying the marketplace

All the explanation you need of how a newspaper or magazine wants you to write is there on paper. It's not that mysterious.

Michelle Griffin, freelance writer

For every journalist or feature writer whose work appears in what we call the mainstream press, there is at least one or two journalists working in what could be called 'corporate communication'. It's the hidden market.

Steve Bright, award-winning corporate journalist

One of the most important skills of writing feature articles is knowing where to send your ideas and stories. Studying the marketplace, or doing your market research, improves your chances of getting into print. Just as your idea for a story must be specific, you should have a particular intended publication in mind—before you pick up a pen to start writing.

The editor's baby

Editors treat their publications as their children—and they know them intimately. Take the time to know a publication, almost as well as its editor, and you will greatly improve your chances of being published. Knowing a publication well, and demonstrating this to the editor, shows that you are thorough, cluey about tailoring your work to an audience and serious about getting published. It's commonsense, courteous, concrete evidence that you are a professional writer. Essentially, you need to know which stories have been published recently, so that you don't double up with your idea; and whether the publication considers stories from freelance writers (known in the trade as contributors). But these are only the basics.

The search begins

The most direct way to study the marketplace is to read the publications you are aiming for from the point of view of a writer, as well as that of a reader. You are aiming to sharpen your focus, to discover what is unique in a particular publication, what sets it apart.

Before studying the stories, locate what we call 'the editorial contact box', where essential details are printed. Here you'll find names, contact numbers, disclaimers and general notes to prospective contributors.

The contents pages will give you a sense of the publication's structure and the interests of its readers.

Now look at the different types of stories in depth: long feature articles, profiles of people and places, instructional stories, lists and so on. As well as developing a sense of the publication's form and content, you should be able to pick up tips for the best way to shape your idea, your story.

Study the articles. Are there precedes (also known as summaries) at the start of many stories? Calculate the word length (also known as the wordage) of the articles. (Work out the average words per line and then multiply by the approximate number of lines in the story.) Check for use of sidebars, postscripts and quizzes: those parts of an article which are not in the main text but add value to the story. Cast a critical eye over the photographs—could you provide photographs of a publishable quality? Keen readers absorb many of these details without needing to take note of them. Keen writers absorb this information and then act upon it.

But there is more to studying a publication than reading its stories. The advertising will tell you a lot about who the magazine thinks its readers are. For example, advertisements for prestige cars can tell you that your idea for an instructional article about basic car maintenance for young drivers is unlikely to suit that magazine. The advertisements, the articles, and the letters page will all give you a wealth of information about the publication's typical readers: their gender, age, income, occupation and interests.

Pat Hayes, editor of camping magazine *On the Road*, comments on the importance of studying the marketplace:

> I expect potential contributors to have read *On the Road*, and to be in touch with the philosophy of the magazine. They should know that our stories do not preach to people, that the tone is one of forming an equal relationship with the readers. Readers think of the magazine as an old friend.
>
> *On the Road* is what I call a 'soft-camping' magazine, so it's no good sending us a story about, say, rock-climbing or mountaineering.
>
> If somebody rings up and asks, 'What sort of story do you want?' then they aren't going to get very far. I don't want a story which is poorly written, or a rewrite of a tourist brochure. Ideally, I want to open up an envelope and find that everything in there is fantastic.

Directories

Media directories such as *Margaret Gee's Australian Media Guide*, *The Australian Writer's Marketplace* and *The Press, Radio and TV Guide* provide an overview of publications throughout Australia. These guides list thousands of Australian media contacts, in daily newspapers, general magazines, trade journals, specialist newsletters and corporate publications. You'll find details on such diverse publications as *Australian Energy News, Transport Worker, Internet World Australia, Australasian Farrier News* and many, many more.

Margaret Gee's Australian Media Guide (Information Australia) is a quarterly publication only available on subscription but some academic libraries have copies in their reference sections. Its target audience is writers, journalists, advertising representatives and public relations consultants.

The annual *The Australian Writer's Marketplace* (Bookman) is directed towards writers of various styles: poets, novelists, screenwriters and freelance non-fiction writers. You should be able to access a copy through local bookshops or perhaps in the reference section of a local library.

The Press, Radio and TV Guide (Media Monitors Australia) is both an annual and monthly publication. Local and academic libraries may have the annual editions and the monthly update is available on subscription. Both cover publications in Australia, New Zealand and the Pacific. It also lists some of the major Asian and US newspapers.

Margaret Gee's Australian Media Guide and *The Australian Writer's Marketplace* both have on-line services available.

The inside information

Contributors' guidelines are available from some publications. These guidelines are a checklist of how the publication prefers to receive material from contributors.

Further afield

There are several more ways of getting to know the marketplace, of finding and perusing potential publications. Talk to people about what non-fiction they read. What are their favourite magazines? Who and what do they like to read

> ## Contributors' guidelines for *The Big Issue*
>
> *The Big Issue* is an independent and commercially viable magazine which publishes quality articles on a huge variety of subjects, including arts and entertainment, lifestyle and profiles. We are always looking for quality writers interested in contributing to our magazine.
>
> We would advise that you read as many copies of *The Big Issue* as possible. This will give you a good idea of the sorts of stories we like and the style of writing we prefer. We are an independent publication and are thus able to do stories other magazines and papers might not be able to do; this is worth keeping in mind . . .
>
> News stories might be as short as 400 words; features usually run between 800 and 2000 words. Length is negotiated between the editor and the writer.
>
> We won't accept stories that have been submitted as part of assessment at any kind of journalism course, unless everyone interviewed for the piece is expressly forewarned that what they told you may be published . . .
>
> We prefer to have articles submitted on disk—saved as a Word document, preferably 5.1 for Macintosh—or e-mailed, but if you don't have access to a computer, we do accept hard copies—by fax or mail . . .
>
> At *The Big Issue* we try to support the quality and professionalism of our content by paying close attention to matters of presentation, style and correctness . . . Our aim is for consistency of style, certainly on each page, ideally throughout each edition and hopefully in the journal in general.

about? What types of articles do they especially like? Talk to your local newsagents. Let them know what you're after, then they can keep an eye out for you.

Pop into newsagents when you are visiting another suburb or city. Visit major public and academic libraries when you get the chance. Broaden your browsing. Read publications

Award-winning corporate journalist Steve Bright comments on opportunities in the corporate world.

> You unpack a new software package. Who wrote the extensive manuals? You see a brochure for a new car, or a newsletter for the Diabetes Association, or a residents' information kit from the local council. Who wrote these?
>
> As with mainstream journalism, the work of the corporate journalist ranges from the simple to the demanding. It also ranges in complexity and creativity. I have written many 'bread and butter' pieces—press releases, brochures, newsletters—but I have also written novels, plays and short stories in the cause of corporate journalism.
>
> A dry annual report can be transformed by a simple line from The Bible, used to engage the reader at the beginning: 'Where there is no vision, the people perish.'
>
> In the past, most corporate journalism was handled through large public relations companies. That's changed in the past decade, with many more freelance writers working independently.
>
> Probably the best thing about corporate journalism (apart from the pay rates, which are often significantly higher than the mainstream press) is the variety.
>
> And it's not all serious—there is room for humour and a sense of adventure. Many people who read corporate writing are very willing to be entertained as well as informed.
>
> The skills you need, beyond good writing, are a capacity to take a brief; having ideas and knowing how to present them; and the ability to work with clients and understand what makes them happy.

which are quite different from your regular reading. Even if the topics don't concern you, the styles of writing should be worth looking at. You may be able to pick up some pointers on sentence length, or paragraph links, or general structure. Check the Internet for web pages of various publications—these will also give you a sample of what's about.

Publication profiles—know your market intimately

A good way to keep track of all the information you gather in your study of the marketplace is to compile a set of publication profiles. This way you develop your knowledge of the market and have the information at your fingertips. What should be in your publication profile? If you complete the following list, you'll have a comprehensive report on a publication you've been studying.

> Title of publication
> Name of editor/feature editor
> Contact details: postal address, phone, fax, e-mail, website
> Frequency of publication: weekly, monthly, quarterly, and so on
> History: number of issues and years in circulation
> Circulation: average number of copies sold
> Distribution: local, state, national, on-line, subscription only
> Contributors: does the publication invite contributions?
> Cover: describe the cover in a word or two: bold? bright? conservative?
> Types of stories: profiles, lists, instructional pieces, and so on
> Length of stories: approximately how many words?
> Tone of the writing: is the writing flamboyant or factual? jokey or jargonistic?
> Advertising: what types of products?
> Readership: your perception of the types of readers of the magazine

Writing down these points articulates your thoughts. You do not have to write a major thesis on the publication; just a series of notes which confirm your understanding of what the marketplace is, of where your story could be sent.

Profiling several publications will help distinguish the differences between them. For example, *Girlfriend* is different from *Dolly*, which is different from *Cleo*, which is different from *New Woman*. All are pitched at women, but different types of women. After a number of profiles you will develop an instinct for what the editor wants and who the readers are.

Build up a collection of the publications you hope to write for. You don't have to buy a heap of issues: just enough so that you can appreciate the finer points of the publications.

Publication profiles can also apply to corporate and community journals. Compare several recent issues of a company's staff magazine. Are the articles long, short, snappy? Has the design changed? Is the language suitable for the readership—there's nothing wrong with jargon, as long as the readers know what the writer is talking about.

Studying the marketplace is part and parcel of being a professional writer. As Rhonda Whitton says, 'Remember that having an article published is not a lottery where, for the price of a stamp, you may win the jackpot and be published' (*The Australian Writer's Marketplace*, Bookman, Melbourne, 1998, p. 2).

Scanning, browsing, reading and perusing publications does not always have to be work at the desk. It's a professional, enjoyable and sometimes addictive habit that can be done over a cup of coffee, on the train, at the beach, in a doctor's waiting room, by the heater on a wet winter's afternoon, with some favourite music playing and the cat curled up on your lap.

Summary

- Visit local newsagents and libraries regularly
- Check websites of publications you would like to write for
- Read from the perspective of a writer, as well as that of a reader
- Look at the advertising and fine print as well as the stories
- Use media guides as much as possible
- Note differences between similar publications

- Read publications that are quite different from your regular reading
- Visit libraries in other cities

Exercises

1. Write about your favourite publication from a reader's point of view. What do you like about it? Why?

2. Write about the same publication from a writer's point of view.

3. Contact the publication and ask if it provides contributors' guidelines.

4. Study the media guides and then answer this short quiz.

    Who is the editor of your favourite supplement in your daily paper?

    What is the circulation of your favourite publication?

    What magazines or newsletters cover your interests and/or your work?

    Name four trade publications.

    Which women's magazines have the biggest circulation?

5. Talk to family, friends and work colleagues about their reading habits. Ask them what they read and why.

6. Compile three publication profiles, one covering a publication that's quite different from your regular reading.

7. Read and compare the two articles about procrastination in appendix 1. How are these stories different, and why? What can you guess about the publications' readers from the stories?

four**Good ideas**

Ideas come from all sorts of places—the skill is in recognising them.
Merran White, freelance writer

Wherever you're aiming to be published, you need a good and steady flow of story ideas before you can start writing. Good story ideas that are well matched with the publication you are aiming at are like money in the bank. Editors are always on the lookout for new and interesting article ideas.

If you want to write feature articles, you need to have an overwhelming sense of curiosity. Writing features gives you the perfect opportunity to go out and interview your favourite DJ on how she got started, to explore the old theatre in your suburb that is being restored to its former glory, to talk to a woman who has started up a new dating service for single people. Writing features is all about satisfying curiosity—yours as well as your readers'.

Still, many beginning writers who want to write feature articles worry that they don't have anything to write about. What they mean is they don't have any ideas they think are good enough, or they have the idea but they get overwhelmed with what to do next. It's not that they don't have the ideas, it's just that they are too critical too early or they have too little confidence in themselves to trust the ideas they do have.

Telling yourself you have no good ideas is guaranteed to give you writer's block. Tell yourself something often enough and deep down you really start to believe it. The reality is that there are a million stories out there, just waiting to be told. What matters is whether or not you are open to them, whether you recognise a story and are excited enough or interested enough to want to tell it.

Once you really start looking at the world around you with writer's eyes, you'll see what we mean. Here are some tips to get you started.

Start with what you know

Everyone's life is unique in some way. Start with your own life experiences. Consider writing about them. It may be a story about travelling with a small child, or passing an important exam, or failing another, or choosing a nursing home for an elderly parent, or surviving a mid-life crisis.

Our students have published first articles on topics as diverse as building a mud brick house, surviving the first day at uni, the benefits of volunteering and getting a journalism cadetship.

Perhaps your working life is a good starting point. Barry Garner's story (see appendix 1) draws heavily on his experiences at work. What about your training—do you have an in-depth knowledge of a topic that you could pass on to a layperson?

Writing about something you know well or have experienced first hand can really build your confidence and it will show in your writing—your story will sound more authoritative.

Move on to who you know

Who could provide you with a good feature story? Develop your networks and let friends and colleagues know that you are on the lookout for good stories.

Perhaps the friend of a friend teaches belly dancing, another has thrown in a long-term career to start up a dog training business, or another has a fascinating story to tell about life as a busker.

Study your market

Aim to write for a particular publication. Get to know it well. Make a conscious decision to look about for stories to write for this publication. You might choose an alternative health magazine, your employer's staff newspaper, or your university newspaper.

Know your readers

Think about the kinds of stories that interest your readers. Consider their daily lives, their worries, preoccupations, what they talk about with their friends, what you think they might be striving for. For a shortcut, look at back issues of a publication to get an idea of what's already been written for these readers—this will give you a clearer picture of what you could write.

Put your ideas antennae up

Driving to the end of your street, listening to the car radio, watching people cross at the lights, construction workers labouring on a new freeway, all of these details flood your senses with information—even though you are engaged in a routine daily activity—driving to work or uni.

With your ideas antennae up you'll find stories at every turn in the road. The radio program you're listening to on smacking children suggests a story on how children are disciplined these days in primary school. Above the freeway you notice a hot air balloon with 'Aerial Photographer' written on the side. You think of a story about different kinds of photography for the education supplement of a daily paper. A well-dressed couple bickering at the tram stop suggests an article on the stresses for couples who work together or a story on family businesses and the advantages and disadvantages of working with other family members for the staff magazine at your work.

Write your ideas down

Writing your ideas down gives you a sense of achievement as well as capturing them before they disappear. Keep an ideas diary or journal.

Treat ideas kindly

Don't knock ideas before they've had a chance to be tested. Write down whatever comes to you—no one's going to be peering over your shoulder. Sort and test them later.

Don't be afraid of odd ideas—popular songs that have brackets in their titles and 50 things you've learned from TV are both ideas that have made their way into print as feature articles.

Don't talk your idea away

Once a story is told it's told. Trying to get it down on paper after you've described it to an interested listener can seem like a real chore. Save the excitement you feel for the story for your reader. Convey your own sense of wonder and fascination about the topic on the page.

Prime your unconscious mind

You may have often woken in the morning just before the alarm's gone off—because the night before you reminded yourself just as you were dropping off to sleep to wake early the next morning. Try using the same trick when it comes to thinking of ideas for stories.

Just as you are dropping off to sleep, tell yourself that you'll wake up with a good story idea in the morning. Or that tomorrow you will have your antennae tuned to potential stories. Keep a pad and pencil handy so that when you wake up you can write down whatever comes to mind.

Try something new

Jolt yourself out of your normal routine and look at the world through the eyes of a writer. Take notice of things around you that you normally pass by. One student wrote an award-winning story about the comings and goings on a typical Saturday night at his all-night corner store—a shop he had been into hundreds of times revealed itself to him as an interesting place to write about.

Visit places you've never been before. Take up an unusual hobby or class. Make a point of reading unfamiliar newspapers or magazines. Take a different route to work or uni. By doing any or all of these things you'll open yourself to new experiences, you'll observe things you're not used to seeing and you'll fuel your imagination.

Look actively for other sources of story ideas

Read the daily paper—daily. And your local paper weekly. Read them from start to finish: news stories, features, letters to the editor, classified advertisements, sport and business pages. This will strengthen your instincts for what makes a good story; it will expose you to a range of writing styles and reveal a heap of potential article ideas.

GOOD IDEAS

Eavesdrop

Listen to what interests your friends, or your potential readers. What are they concerned about? What gets them interested? What information or services do they need? Have you noticed any trends among them—roller blading, divorce ceremonies, anything—that you can identify and write about?

Read specialist publications

Specialist publications, such as journals or newsletters, will be written for the person who shares some knowledge of the subject. Try looking at some of the topics covered from a layperson's point of view. With your skills in writing plain, punchy and effective English you can turn academic, dry, technical or wordy articles into interesting stories.

Watch out for upcoming conferences

When experts congregate together they often talk the same language—one that is inaccessible to the general public. Use your writing skills to translate a good story complete with interviews from visiting world experts.

Browse at the library

Spend time in the non-fiction section of your library—there's a goldmine of ideas for stories here which could be revisited in a shorter format or which could lead you to ideas for other stories.

Listen to the radio

Choose a radio station you don't normally listen to and keep pencil and paper handy. You'll notice that radio, TV and print 'borrow' story ideas from each other all the time. You'll be mining the radio for ideas that you can put a different angle on and write about.

Collect brochures and pamphlets

Collect them at the doctor, the dentist, or at your child's school. A pamphlet on how to deal with a child who is stealing could be the starter for an interesting series of interviews with experts on how to deal with a range of common but troubling childhood behaviours aimed at a parents' magazine. Or it could jog a memory from your own past that you could write about.

Look at the calendar

What anniversaries or events are coming up that you could write about? The anniversary of Kurt Cobain's/Michael Hutchence's death? Chinese New Year? National Stutterers' Week?

Surf the Internet

Use the Internet to spawn story ideas. A listing of clubs suggests an article on the longest running/weirdest/most popular clubs in your state—Reptile Club, Nudist Club, Homing Pigeon Club, Scrabble Club. Or the home page of an animal therapist suggests an article on people in odd jobs.

Select which ideas to write about

It's important to put all ideas you have down on paper first. Selecting them comes later. By the time you've completed all the exercises in this chapter you'll have a stack of ideas in your notebook. Consider these questions when you are choosing which ones to write about.

1. Am I interested enough in it to write about it? If you're not interested in a topic it'll be hard to interest your readers.

2. Is it likely to interest my readers? Would somebody else want to read this? You may be passionately interested in

the feeding habits of the aardvark but it might not be of much interest to anyone else. Except of course unless you are writing for a zoology magazine!

3. Can I afford to write this story? This is a very practical consideration. Unless you have a working relationship with an editor that includes expenses, you will have to be responsible for any costs you incur in writing your story: long-distance telephone calls, faxes, travel and so on. Also consider whether you have the time to spend on such a story.

4. Is there a good market for it? Can you identify a publication that would be likely to buy this story? Study the market and match your story to the publication you are aiming at.

5. Is the idea specific enough? Or would it be better as a book? An article on a subject such as elephants, for example, is too broad. Narrow the subject down into a more specific angle. You might narrow it down to working elephants or circus elephants or how they are trained, or how Asian elephant numbers are declining. And again, you'd have to narrow the focus. You might write about the oldest elephant in Australia, or holidays on elephants or the role of elephants in Sri Lanka's Kandy Perahera Festival.

6. Has the idea been done before? You might want to write about romances on the Internet. But when you do a bit of research you find it's been done to death. Perhaps you could write about divorces on the net.

Congratulate yourself when someone beats you to it

There's no copyright on story ideas. Often writers get very discouraged when the story idea they're excited about turns up, written by someone else, in the pages of a magazine or newspaper. Yes, it's disappointing that someone else got to it first, but doesn't it demonstrate that you've got a nose for a good story? And by now there are plenty more ideas where that one came from.

Merran White studied psychology and politics and edited the student newspaper at Melbourne University. After a number of media courses, she joined Cosmopolitan as a copyeditor in 1987 and progressed to production manager, senior features and entertainment editor. In 1990 she began freelancing. She writes for marie claire, Elle, Studio, Cosmopolitan, Cleo, Reader's Digest, Australian Style, and Time Out and Company—both UK magazines. Her latest book is Going Solo: a Guide for Women Travelling Alone.

Start with what you know, what you're good at, interested in or interested in finding out more about. If you're a woman at home with children, then you could start with parenting. There's no fun in writing about things you're not interested in. Look around your life and ask yourself what you are passionate about, and use that to generate ideas.

The globalisation of the media means that every idea has been done before, in one form or another, especially in women's magazines. Ask yourself what can you bring that's new or different to an old idea.

Ideas come to me when I'm chatting, or having dinner with friends or reading the paper and the idea I have ties in with a whole bunch of things I've been thinking about. 'There's a story in this,' I often say to myself.

I look out for things that generate enthusiasm in other people. 'Can you afford your boyfriend?' If every woman I say this to laughs then there is an idea in it. Talk to 'normal' people—people in shops, people who aren't in your circle—and find out what they are concerned or worried about.

I brainstorm ideas. I sit and write down as many ideas for stories as I can think of. I don't censor myself. Then I think about where I can place them. It's interesting to watch how many of your article ideas come up in the contents pages over a six-month period.

You've got to read newspapers, magazines. Sometimes a newspaper item will leap out at you and it'll have story written all over it. Look at the contents pages, look for trends. Read widely so you don't turn in on yourself. Read the best and read the publications you want to write for.

When I get an idea I actually think, Is this story going to do anyone any good? I like to think they've got some useful content.

Keep a contact book. Never throw out a phone number. You never know when you'll need it for a future story.

It's also in the company you keep. I've got friends who are mothers, tradespeople, young people, old people, lawyers, media people, financiers, students, artists. I take a GP friend to lunch sometimes when I need to talk about a story and last time he talked about how many people he'd seen who were worried about their kids' asthma. I thought, there's a story in that.

Summary
- Start with what you know
- Move on to who you know
- Study your market
- Put your ideas antennae up
- Write your ideas down
- Treat ideas kindly
- Don't talk your idea away
- Prime your unconscious mind
- Try something new
- Look actively for other sources of story ideas
- Select which ideas to write about
- Congratulate yourself when someone beats you to it

Exercises

1. Make a short list of things that you have recently learned to do or some specialist knowledge that you have that you could write about. It could be anything from choosing a nursing home for an elderly relative to building a barbeque to organising a children's party.

2. Imagine you are a visitor from overseas coming to your town for the weekend. Go to your local museum or art gallery, have lunch at a popular tourist spot, try to look at your town with a visitor's eyes. Make a note of what stories you could write from this experience.

3. Sit down with your weekend paper and read it. Take note of any story ideas that suggest themselves to you as you read. Your aim is to come up with as many story ideas as you can. Don't discard any at this stage.

4. Read the classified ads section of your papers. Is there a new service being advertised? An ad for a bridal gown '$800 and never worn' that gets you wondering about the whole business of people being jilted? Add these to your ideas list.

5. Read a professional journal or newsletter from a community group. Note down any ideas for future issues that occur to you in your reading.

6. Clip ten travel stories from newspapers and magazines. Describe the specific angle of each story in a sentence or two.

7. Find someone with an interesting story to tell. It can be a VIP in your local community, or someone with an unusual job or hobby. Write down what sorts of things you and your readers would like to know about them.

8. Write for twenty minutes without stopping about a turning point in your life.

9. Choose one idea from your journal or ideas diary that you think will interest a reader. Write about it for fifteen minutes without stopping.

five Types of articles

Generally I'm looking for a point well made, and an enjoyable journey in getting to that point.

Jim Buckell, former editor, Time & Tide page, *The Australian*

Part of narrowing down a story idea is working out what type of article suits that idea. What is the best way to present your story?

You've narrowed down a story idea from the general topic of travel to travelling and holidaying with young children. But in what format, what style, will you write that story? As a profile, a list, an instructional article? Or in another way?

Using travelling with young children as a story idea, let's look at the various types of non-fiction articles you could write:

- a profile of a world travelling family
- an as-told-to account of sailing around the world with young children
- an instructional/how-to story on keeping the children entertained during an interstate trip
- an A to Z of tips for people travelling overseas with young children

- a top ten list of children-friendly winter getaways in your state
- a news feature looking at holiday farms
- an anecdotal account of a humorous incident while holidaying with young children
- a promotional (advertorial) piece promoting family-oriented bed-and-breakfast accommodation in your region
- a comment piece on parents who are too busy to take their children on holidays
- a review of some travel books about travelling with children

Whatever your idea, whatever your angle, there are various types of articles to suit. Each type has a distinct structure, a way of shaping the material. Let's have a brief look at these types of articles.

Profiles

Personality profiles can be 800-word snapshots or, in the hands of Walkley Award winner Janet Hawley, intimate insights of several thousand words into the lives of public figures.

Profiles contain a mix of factual information, anecdotal stories illustrating a person's life and quotes, certainly from the person being profiled and often from friends and colleagues of the person.

Profiles often start with paragraphs about a recent incident or issue involving the person and then, sometimes as late as halfway through, basic biographical information may be supplied in chronological order. The story then makes its way back to the present day and will often return to what is currently newsworthy about the person. That 'currency' may tie in with an anniversary of some kind, a new book about the person, the person's recovery from serious illness or a concert tour.

Encapsulating part of a person's life with just a few thousand words offers the writer the opportunity to construct a narrative style of writing. Essentially, you are presenting a series of stories and reflections.

Profiles of people do not appear in just mainstream magazines. Specialist publications (boating, hi-fi, whatever) run profiles of experts in their areas, adding a human element to the person's technical expertise. See the stories by Paul Daffey and Rob Doole in appendix 1 for examples of profile articles.

Travel profiles

A travel profile is a piece that goes beyond merely promoting a favourite place. It tells stories about the place, and about the people who live there, or used to live there. It creates impressions and images of the place, words and ideas that go past what you read in travel brochures.

A travel profile takes all the clichés and sees if they really are true. It tries to look at things a little differently. As a keen observer you will pick up on aspects of a place which are left out in the glossy brochures. The good travel writer will impart a sense of the place. Facts and figures are important, of course, but a travel profile is often about mood and atmosphere, about taking the reader there and providing a glimpse of the place. And it's about telling stories—odd historical anecdotes, paragraph-length portraits of local characters and amusing observations.

As-told-to stories

These are the stories in which the writer interviews a person and then writes up the story in the first person, the 'I' being not the writer but the person who has been interviewed. These articles require very sound quoting, for the article is in fact presented as one long, uninterrupted quote. Quotes may need to be shifted about to create a better series of links between paragraphs. Some sentences may need to be carefully reworded to avoid grammatical entanglements.

When the entire article is one long quote the writer has to sew things together seamlessly. Your role is to record, rather than to interpret. You must make the person sound as natural as possible. There is no room for you to add adverbs or adjectives or descriptions of body language, clothing, setting. At the most, you may have a short opening paragraph to set the scene. After that, the words must speak for themselves.

Instructional articles

Instructional articles (or how-to articles) show a reader how to do something. The possibilities are endless. You can write instructional articles on cooking a Christmas roast, pruning an apple tree, building a pergola, getting fit, making a letterbox, fixing a flat tyre.

Your first instructional articles need to be about a subject you know about. You may be very good at Japanese cooking or training dogs or building letterboxes. This first-hand knowledge is a vital resource for writing an instructional piece.

Order is everything in these types of articles. Put things in the order they are in real life. State the obvious, because the reader is not expected to be as knowledgeable as yourself. Use simple language but don't talk down to the reader. A recipe is a prime example of an instructional article. It is absolutely necessary to get every fact, every figure, every instruction correct. There's a big difference between a tablespoon and a teaspoon of baking soda.

An instructional article can range from 200 words to about 1000, depending on the complexity of the topic. Accompanying photographs are handy with this type of article, especially for DIY topics.

Once you have developed some confidence in writing in this style, you could try your hand at covering slightly unfamiliar topics. You do not have to be an expert in the area, though some interest does help. A good non-fiction writer, like a good reporter, can collect information from an expert and then pass it on in terms the reader understands.

List articles

You will find list articles just about everywhere: Top Tens, Top 100s, A to Zs. Editors love list articles because they know readers can't resist them. List articles offer readers the chance to learn things quickly, or to disagree with the list. (A list of, say, great fast bowlers, is bound to cause some discussion.)

List articles are particularly popular over the easy-reading period of the Christmas/New Year holidays. The end of the year is ripe for articles listing achievements of the year, albums of the year, books of the year, quotes of the year, and so on.

List articles are especially enjoyable if fact-finding is your forte. Some list articles are very quirky: the Greatest B-Sides of All Time; an A to Z of Lawn-mowing; Hit Songs with Brackets in Their Titles.

Not all list articles are light, and not all are simply A to Zs or Top Tens. There have been list articles with short profiles of unsung heroes and of up-and-coming artists. There have also been list articles about various illnesses.

The reference section of your local library is a good starting point for looking for ideas for list articles and also for researching such articles.

A tip on compiling an A to Z list—make sure you can cover those tricky letters, in particular, Q, X, Y and Z.

See 'How to stop putting it off' by Gina Perry in appendix 1 for an example of a list and instructional article.

News feature stories

These stories present an issue or a breakthrough or a trend. The issue of the millenium bug led to many feature articles and books. The changing role of men in modern society, for example, has led to many feature stories quoting psychologists and family therapists.

A news feature story delves behind the initial news story. It goes into more detail about the what, when and where of a story and then asks questions about the how and why. Like a personality profile, it may begin with the immediate newsworthy aspect and then go backwards a little, filling in details in chronological order before returning to the main issue.

Promotional articles

Promotional articles (known in the industry as advertorials) are a form of advertising. They are promotions for products, presented as feature articles within an advertising supplement. The term 'advertorial' combines 'advertisement' with 'editorial', traditionally the two separate parts of a publication.

A newspaper, for example, may run a two-page spread, called an 'advertising feature', about educational opportunities for school leavers. The pages will be financed by advertisements for universities and colleges. There will also be some articles that look like typical newspaper stories.

First-person articles

Anecdotes

An anecdote, or vignette, is a short, personal story. They are either light and breezy or intimate and revealing. These stories rarely run beyond 1000 words and usually require a keen sense of narrative, of telling a story with a beginning, a middle and an end. They offer chances for humour and/or poignancy. Most writers have at least a handful of publishable anecdotes to tell: a reflection on the passing seasons, a humorous domestic incident, a study of the characters on the morning train, the day a parent or close friend died.

A good writer of anecdotes will strike a common chord with readers, not just once, but over and over again. Such writers are sometimes offered regular spots—columns—and develop a type of pen-friend relationship with thousands of readers.

Many writers think that anecdotal writing is easy because they're, usually, writing about material they know well—themselves. But anecdotal pieces require much discipline. One of the keys to writing anecdotes is to remember that the story is more important than yourself. Keep asking yourself, Will this interest anybody else? My story means a lot to me, but why should it mean a lot to others? See 'Dog days' by Barry Garner and 'Bourke to Collins: tales of the city' by Deborah Forster, both in appendix 1, for examples of anecdotes.

Comment pieces

Comment pieces give the non-fiction writer the chance to present an opinion on a topic. They must be topical, tackling a current news issue. They must also be well argued, logically presented, and backed up with facts and, possibly, quotes. Comment pieces are not usually the domain of novice writers. An editor is more likely to run a comment piece by an expert. A comment piece is akin to a good essay: the writer has something to say, and says it well.

Reviews

Reviews are, by definition, subjective but the praise or condemnation must still be backed up with a knowledge of the

> *Jim Buckell has been a journalist for twenty years. Most recently he was editor of the Time & Tide page of* The Australian, *which includes* Observer, *a column mainly written by contributors. He gives us an insider's view of the Observer column.*
>
> The essence of the Observer stories is that they are reflective and written in the first person. I'm usually looking for astute observations of topical events.
>
> A highly personal piece can work too but it's got to be very good. Some writers think that stories about their families are going to be interesting, but they're usually boring. You've got to have a special take on a family incident to make such a story work. Sometimes I run a more classically styled essay piece which may collect various quotes and ideas on a topic as it makes its point, usually of an abstract or philosophical nature.
>
> A safe starting point for ideas for the Observer column is to write about something that's in the news, and to look at the implications of that issue. Generally, I'm looking for a point well made, and an enjoyable journey in getting to that point. I know within the first three paragraphs whether a story will cut the mustard. If the story is not quite good enough but I sense it's worth perservering with, I'll ask the writer to do a rewrite. This may require tightening up a passage, avoiding going off on a tangent, and keeping your eyes on the prize.

subject, with references to the technical and thematic aspects of whatever is being reviewed. Word length ranges from snappy ten-word quips to 200-word reviews to 5000-word essays that you'll find in literary magazines.

All sorts of things can be reviewed: books, compact discs, concerts, exhibitions, festivals, movies, products, restaurants, theatre, TV programs, websites, wine. Writing reviews for a student paper, a community newsletter or staff newsletter is a good way to practice brevity. It also gives you room to develop a personal style.

Remember that it is possible for reviews to be defamatory (see appendix 2), so make sure you can back up your opinions with facts.

Summary

- There are many topics and ideas for articles but only a handful of types of articles
- Different types of articles require different structures
- Profile pieces can be about places as well as people
- Choose a topic you know about when trying your first instructional articles
- Watch out for those troublesome consonants in A to Z lists
- News feature stories delve deeper than a straight news story, going into the how and why of an issue, a breakthrough or a trend
- Promotional pieces are a form of advertising
- Make sure your anecdotal story is worth telling
- Comment pieces are usually the domain of experts
- Writing reviews for small publications is a good exercise in brevity and developing a personal style

Exercises

1. Read the stories in appendix 1. What types of articles are they?

2. Read a handful of your favourite publications and identify the different types of stories. Can you find a category that we haven't covered?

3. Choose one of your article ideas and describe different ways of writing it: as a profile, an instructional piece, a news feature, and so on.

4. Write instructional pieces on these topics: changing a flat tyre, hosting a children's party, preparing for final high school exams.

5. Compile an A to Z or Top Ten of a favourite topic.

6. Write a short (300-word) review of a concert, CD, book or something else. Compare it to a published review of the same topic.

7. Try your hand at an anecdotal piece about a first day—in a new job, in a new home or in a foreign country, for example.

six**Research**

To me, history has always been about telling stories. I love uncovering stories—whether of places or people. It never ceases to amaze me how varied and fascinating such stories are. I love talking to people who have a passion for a particular place or person. Their enthusiasm is invariably infectious.

Mary Ryllis Clark, freelance writer

A good feature is something that tells you something you didn't know before. It's a story that has surprising characters. Ours is an issues-based magazine, but the writers have to get people into their stories. We receive some articles that are full of research and facts but there's no human face. A good feature is about making strangers connect.

Thornton McCamish, editor, *The Big Issue*

Creativity is something you need at every stage in writing a feature article. And research, too, is a step that requires you to use your imagination and think laterally. You also need perseverance and patience as well as good fact-finding skills.

Be prepared to leave the cosiness of your room. Research means hitting the road (and the information superhighway) with your notebook and pencil in hand and your observation skills at the ready. It means talking, reading, asking questions, taking notes, watching and listening. In the tradition of the hard news story, you need to get out there and find out the who, what, when, where, why and how of your story. These are the essential building blocks of your feature. Use them to guide your research.

Research gives flesh and blood to the bones of your article idea. Your research should gather a combination of factual information, words from real people and short stories or incidents that illustrate or develop your theme. These elements can be obtained from organisations and from people as well as from published material.

For many, research is the most interesting part of writing a feature—they enjoy the chance to get out there and ask questions about something they've always wanted to know more about and enjoy becoming involved in a subject in ways that they may not have experienced before. Others are often daunted by the prospect of research because they mistakenly believe that you need to be an academic to do it well. Or they worry that people won't talk to them and give them information if all the writer's got is an idea and no firm committment from an editor. Others believe that research is boring, it's writing that interests them, and research seems like a waste of time.

The truth is that research can involve all the drama, tension and hard-slogging footwork of a good detective story. You start with a question or a hunch and, in tracking down answers, you are led down many interesting and surprising alleys and a fair few dead-end streets. Ultimately, though, it's worth it for an interesting and accurate story.

In finding things out, you talk to people who know a lot about the topic you're interested in. You get to meet people who are happy to share their enthusiasm for the subject. Don't apologise for being a newcomer, just show your interest and you'll be amazed at how willing people are to share information. Be clear about what you plan to do with the information they give you and where you hope to have it published. You'll find most people appreciate your interest and candour and will be more than happy to help you.

Effective research homes in on the information you need—use the phone and the Internet to establish where you need to go to follow things up. Yes, research will take more time than the writing of an article but if you've done it well you'll find the writing is easier. You should also find that you have far more material than you need, material that you can use in future articles or story ideas.

Research is fun. You get to meet new people and to put yourself out there as a new writer gathering information for a story. Without your facts, quotes and anecdotes you haven't got a credible story. A well-researched story makes your writing more confident because you know what you're talking about and it gives your writing authority.

Your angle dictates your research

The angle you take on a particular topic will determine the kind and amount of research you do. Take the Austudy examples from chapter 1. The list article on the top ten opportunity shops for students will require you to do quite different research than the profile of three students and how they survive on their income.

Where you get your information from will also affect how objective your story is. For example, if you are doing a story on the effect of tourists on the Great Barrier Reef and you only interview a tour operator, your story will be biased. Remember to interview people from both sides of any story, if there are two or more views on the topic. If, on the other hand, you are doing a straightforward factual story about the restoration of your local cinema, you need only interview the architect in charge of the restoration.

Types of research

Observation

Observational research is a way of using your own observations in a story. Focus on gathering detail, and in particular sensory information. Look at Deborah Forster's story in appendix 1 as a good example of this.

Reading

Read what's already been published on the subject either in printed or electronic form. Books, brochures, magazines or manuals, newsletters, newspapers and journals—look widely for reading material on your topic.

Interviewing

The interview is your main source of research. Stories need people and that means interviews. Interviews can be straight information gathering or fact checking; they can be by phone or face to face; they can can be short and sharp, or long and in-depth.

Interview those people who have the authority to talk on the subject, experts and those closely involved. If you're writing about diabetes in pregnancy, you won't interview your nextdoor neighbour about it. You'd seek out experts, specialist doctors to talk about the causes and treatment of diabetes during pregnancy. Of course, if your nextdoor neighbour is a sufferer you may well interview her for a personal perspective from someone closely involved in or affected by the illness. Contact professional organisations representing the group/individual you want to speak to. Confirm with the person that they are the expert on this topic.

Participating

Some stories lend themselves well to participation as a form of research. Participant observation is research that involves you in participating in the story you are writing as well as observing it. For example, you may join a belly dancing class or take a guided tour all in the name of research.

Talking and eavesdropping

Listening to what other people have to say about your interview subject or the topic itself can give you background, feedback and help you measure interest in the subject.

Sources for research

Libraries

Libraries have not yet been superseded by cyberspace. The two are compatible. If you can't find something at the library, try the Internet, or vice versa. Many libraries now have Internet access. For a fee, university libraries will give you access to interlibrary loans. Kinds of libraries include:

- public: local, state
- educational: school, TAFE, university
- corporate: corporations, business groups or special interest groups
- specialist: usually attached to government departments or universities

Internet

A cautionary word: The Internet can be fascinating but time consuming. It can be a fantastic research tool but make sure you use credible material. As well as the content of the material, check author details. Is the author named? Is he or she an authoritative source?

How current is the information? Check when the material was last revised or updated.

Professional organisations and associations, self-help groups

These can provide spokespeople and experts on the topic, whether it be an Alzheimers group, a sporting body or a teachers' union.

Telephone directories

Directories are a good starting point for contacts. They are particularly useful for listings of government departments and local authorities.

Government authorities

Authorities often have brochures and other printed material available that could be helpful in research. They may also employ information officers.

University faculties

Universities can provide information about experts in the field you are researching and provide background material for your topic.

Research rules

Keep an open mind

Research means testing your ideas with evidence. You may discover in the course of the research that your initial hunch is wrong and that you have to pursue another tack. You'll find many unexpected twists and turns in the road.

Be organised and accurate

Write down the names, job titles and phone numbers of all people you speak to on the information trail. Keep all your material in one folder. Always check material twice. Verify material from secondary sources. For example, if you find a magazine article that says 55 new female jockeys have been registered in the first quarter of 1999, check this figure with the body that registers them.

Know when to stop

Research can be addictive. Knowing when to stop is just as important as making a start. Stop when you've got a lot more material than you need. Stop when your research feels finished and when you feel ready to put pen to paper or fingers to keyboard. Stop when you know you've got more than enough to cover what you want to say. Beware of using research as an excuse to avoid writing.

> **RESEARCH CASE STUDY: WOMEN JOCKEYS**
>
> You go to the races one afternoon and notice on the list of the day's jockeys there is only one woman's name. You want to write an article looking at women jockeys. You don't know much about the topic, but you're very interested in it, and the spring racing season is coming up. You think this story would be suitable for the sports pages of a Sunday newspaper. Your research plan looks something like this:
>
> - You need some hard facts on the numbers of women jockeys over time. After all, you have to verify that your hunch is correct, that there are more now than there were ten years ago.
> - Next you want to know a bit about what the life of a jockey involves, the reasons why more women are going into it, what training is required and whether or not they are in demand. You can get all this information, you hope, from a peak body that represents jockeys.
> - For colour and anecdotes you'd like to profile three women jockeys.

> *Research involved*
>
> Find **background information** in a **library**. Look at the careers section in the library, and find a brochure or reference book on careers that provides details of the training, personal qualities, and aptitudes required to be a jockey. The brochure may outline that jockeys need to be registered with a registration board and may provide a phone number. You can also do a search of newspapers via CD-ROM for previous articles on women jockeys or women in racing.
>
> Ring the **professional organisation** that registers jockeys in your state, explain what you want and ask for the most appropriate person to speak to. Check the numbers of women jockeys registered in your state in the current year, and five or even ten years ago. Ask the person to comment on the numbers. Ask for a contact or contacts for an interview.
>
> **Watch** a jockey or jockeys at work. Attend an early morning track work session or watch them at the races. Take notes on what you observe, including sensory detail and information that brings the story to life and gives colour to the piece by conveying the feel or atmosphere of a place.
>
> **Talk** to anyone you know who is keen on racing about women jockeys to get a feel for perceptions of women jockeys.
>
> Make a **checklist of questions** that you will ask the women jockeys you **interview**. Remember to include factual information too, such as their age, how long they've been riding, and so on.
>
> Accept that this stage will feel chaotic—you will be overloaded with information if you are researching well.

Research leads to more story ideas

One of the exciting things about research is that it spawns new article ideas. For example, you discover in your interview with one jockey that she has come from a long line of jockeys. You get interested in a story on racing families.

In uncovering information on your topic you'll find lots

of other interesting stories and ideas. Some you'll pursue, others you won't. Write them all down for a later date. Enjoy it. It's one of the unexpected and exciting aspects of research.

Research forces you to participate in things in a way that you may not have done before. It's often stimulating, always interesting and sometimes frustrating. And, done well, it's the substance, the nuts and bolts of your story. For without the facts, the quotes and the anecdotes, there is no story, only an idea, a hunch or an observation. These may be all you need if you want to write a short piece based on your own experiences, but even then you need to have been up close, gathering detail and material from your own observations.

Remember, your research—the kind and amount—will be determined by the type of feature article you're doing. What's common to all features is that you start by writing down your thoughts on the topic. You can call this a predraft, if you like. It helps you to sort out your thinking—you ask yourself questions, highlight facts that need checking and identify gaps in your knowledge that need filling.

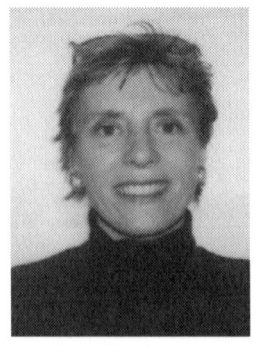

Mary Ryllis Clark read history at London University and worked in publishing in the UK before emigrating to Melbourne in 1980. She started a new career as a freelance writer and editor in 1986. She writes material for historical exhibitions, books, and feature and travel stories. Mary has been writing her fortnightly Historic Victoria column for the travel pages of the Age since 1992. Here Mary Ryllis Clark talks about researching the McCrae homestead. (See 'Georgiana's passion' in appendix 1.)

I do some research in advance before visiting a historic site I am planning to write about—how old it is, who lived there, why it is significant and so on. I then go there to get a sense of the place itself. I talk to local people who are involved with it. For example, with the McCrae homestead story I went 'round the property with one of the voluntary guides who showed me the wonderful family possessions there. The paintings done by Georgiana give a great sense of what it was like before the suburbs grew up around the property.

I read Georgiana's journals, I went to the National Trust files and read up on the reports on the house and the McCrae collection. I also read Brenda Niall's book *Georgiana*. As I like to add direct quotes in stories, I rang Brenda and talked to her about Georgiana and the homestead.

I like places like McCrae because there are two aspects to the story—the place and the people. Having a personal angle to a story always makes it more attractive. The resources I use are the state library, the National Trust, local libraries and my own reference books. I find small, local histories invaluable. Also talking to local historians or people associated with the local historical society, museums and so on.

I also have a good relationship with a number of people who are experts in their field and who are generous enough to share their knowledge in the interests of getting things right and making a place known.

To do research well you need to know where to go for the right information. If not, you need to know who to ask to point you in the right direction. There is a tremendous amount of goodwill out there. Tap into it. Find an expert but don't expect him or her to do the work for you. They will be happy to give you a good quote but will expect you to do some of the legwork.

Summary

- Think of research as a detective story
- Your angle dictates the research you do
- Types of research include:
    observation
    reading

    interviewing
    participating
    talking and eavesdropping
- Research sources include:
    libraries
    the Internet
    professional organisations and associations, self-help groups
    telephone directories
    government authorities
    personal contacts
    university faculties
- Research rules will help you gain and sort knowledge:
    keep an open mind
    be organised and accurate
    know when to stop

Exercises

1. Observe the person sitting next to you for twenty seconds. Now turn away and write down a much as you can about what they are wearing.

2. Do the same exercise with a photograph.

3. Look at four articles in appendix 1, including Mary Ryllis Clark's. List all the research that each writer did for each story.

4. Identify an anecdote in each of the four articles you look at.

5. The case study in this chapter outlined the research involved in a story on the growth in numbers of women jockeys. What research would you do for a story on how apprentice jockeys are selected for the job?

6. You want to interview the following people. Write a sentence or two about how you'd go about finding them:
   a magician
   an airline pilot
   an emu farmer who's gone broke

7. Spend a day in your state library. Familiarise yourself with the reference collection, computer catalogue, newspaper files and Internet access. What print indexes and electronic indexes are available? List the available CD-ROM products that might be useful to you as a writer of feature articles.

8. Now that you are so familiar with your library, try this quiz.

   > What is the name of the chancellor at the university closest to your home?
   >
   > Where and when was your favourite writer born?
   >
   > How many international tourists visited your state last year?
   >
   > Name two specialist and two university libraries in your state.
   >
   > Who is the chairperson of the Australia Council?
   >
   > What is the name of the oldest pub in the capital city nearest you?
   >
   > What professional bodies look after the interests of journalists, screenwriters and writers in general?

9. The windows of your local bookshop are crammed with ads for people wanting housemates. You want to write a story on how people choose new housemates for a university newspaper. List the people you might interview, places you might go and things you might do to gather

background information for this story. Be specific. Describe how you would find this information.

10. You've always been intrigued by the kind of people who work as tattooists. You're planning a story on the kind of people who do it. List the people you might interview, places you might go and things you might do to gather background information for this story. Be specific. Describe how you would find this information.

11. You're interested in the growth of the personal service industry—the house cleaners, personal trainers and pet therapists who make up an increasing part of our economy. After some thought, you hone in on one group, personal trainers, because one has opened a business near your work and every time you pass you see a steady stream of clients entering or leaving the building. List the people you might interview, places you might go and things you might do to gather background information for this story. Be specific. Describe how you would find this information.

sevenInterviewing

It is a privilege to interview someone, not a right.

Janet Hawley, Gold Walkley Award winner

I believe the journalist and the person being interviewed both have to give something of themselves to make it a good story.

Brian Nankervis, actor, author

Interviewing is a little like fishing—you're the angler casting out for answers and hoping to reel in some good material for your story: factual information; quotes that give character to a story; and anecdotes, those little stories which often strike a chord with readers.

Interviews can be conducted personally (face to face), over the phone, via the fax or through e-mail. This chapter deals mainly with interviewing face to face.

Background briefing

The key to a good interview is preparation. It is a matter of professional courtesy to be well read and well prepared, to have questions that are relevant, succinct, perhaps off-beat without being frivolous.

Interviews are part of research so you will already have some information about the person or topic you're researching. An interviewee will respond well if you can show that you have done some background work.

Arranging questions

A good set of questions is like a good roadmap. It shows you how to get from A to B and what to do if there are any detours.

Your questions will help you to fill in gaps in the research and to expand on already-known points. You will have 'closed' questions, which will elicit straight, factual answers, and 'open' questions, which should generate more animated responses.

Save tough questions for later in the interview, when some rapport has been established. If you're keen to ask especially probing questions, be prepared for challenging, perhaps abrupt, answers. Avoid dull questions. They can only lead to dull answers.

You will want a few more questions than you need, but not so many that the interview turns into an interrogation. A personality profile of 1500 words should not need more than a dozen questions.

Making the appointment

Always plan well ahead. A prospective interviewee may not be available for days or weeks. The interviewee will want some basic details: what's your article about? what publication is it for? how much time will it take? You should be able to present these details when you make initial contact (whether that be by phone, fax or e-mail). Inform your interviewee if the interview will be tape recorded and ask for permission to have photographs taken.

Case study

Here's the story: the local gravedigger is retiring after a lifetime of burying people. He could be a good character for a short—800 word—profile. You haven't met the man before but you have heard that he can be a bit surly. You sense there are stories to be told, it's just a matter of eliciting them from the gravedigger. You phone him at the cemetery and, despite his reluctance, you arrange a time to get together. At the cemetery—on his turf.

After 50 years of anonymity, the prospect of being in the paper is a little daunting to him. You have overcome his reluctance by convincing him that his story is worth telling, that he must have a unique perspective on death and burial. You've also suggested he may have some amusing anecdotes that people would like to read about. It turns out he is not so much surly, as shy, a man who thinks he has done his job well if he is not noticed. The closed questions could include:

> How long have you been digging graves? Or, When did you start digging graves? (You're looking for some specific facts, for instance, 1949, or August 1949.)
>
> How did you get started in this type of work?
>
> How many graves do you think you would have dug over the years? (You're not looking for an exact figure here.)
>
> What was the first grave you dug? What was the last? (These questions could frame the story well.)

The open questions seek to encourage anecdotes, little stories.

> Can you recall your first day on the job?
>
> What's the best/worst/funniest/saddest part of being a grave digger? Ask these questions separately—not all at once! Each of these questions should trigger at least one anecdote each.
>
> How has grave-digging changed over the years?

> What did this cemetery look like when you started?
>
> How would you like to be buried? What would you want on your gravestone?
>
> How will you be spending your retirement?
>
> What advice do you have for anyone contemplating a career like yours?

Where to interview

Choosing a venue for the interview is generally a matter of letting the interviewee decide: their home, their office, wherever. Avoid places that are likely to be especially noisy (cafes during peak hour for example).

Brian Nankervis is an actor, author and television warm-up man. He is best known for his alter-ego, the poet Raymond J. Bartholomeuz. He has been interviewed 'hundreds of times' and also interviewed many people for his book about men and sport, Boys and Balls *(Allen & Unwin, Sydney, 1994).*

I believe the journalist and the person being interviewed both have to give something of themselves to make it a good story. If the journo has made obvious mistakes, like getting facts wrong or not having read press releases, then the interview will be hopeless. Also, I don't like people who are really fawning in their praise.

The best interviews are when someone comes from a different angle or exhibits true understanding and a passion for what I do. The best interviewers will always hit you with a question you don't expect and perhaps go off on a tangent. Bert Newton's good at that.

Basically, you need somewhere quiet for an interview. I like doing phone interviews while at home. I don't like being interviewed in cafes—it's predictable, trendy and there are too many distractions. An interview at home can be invasive although I can see how a good journalist will use that setting to get some scene-setting and background material.

I don't mind e-mail interviews. It gives you time to construct something. But I spend too much time on a handful of questions. Hours!

It's annoying and frustrating being misquoted. I was once completely misquoted in a story about warm-up people. The journo asked me the hoary old question about warm-up people being underrated. I replied that there are more important jobs, like teaching, which are underrated. When the story came out it said 'Nankervis believes that warm-up people are underrated', which is the exact opposite of what I said. It was as if the journo had his own agenda and wanted me to say what he wanted to say.

There are some journalists who ring back and check things, which is great. Seeing a story before it is printed is handy because sometimes things are misheard or the journalist gets the wrong end of the stick. The main thing is that a journalist checks for accuracy.

Dress and appearance

You may work from home and sit at your desk in old jeans, a holey jumper and your favourite runners. When you're out interviewing, however, dress appropriately and you are more likely to establish rapport. Turn up in your old jeans and runners and you may find the interviewee less than accommodating. Use your professional judgement. You must be comfortable in what you wear but also recognise you may be judged by appearances.

Punctuality

Be early so you can check your notes and tape recorder. Be early so you can make observations about the subject's home and neighbouring area, business office, the weather, the feel of the day. Sometimes it can give you just the right opening to the interview.

Those first few minutes

This can be the trickiest part of the interview. Don't launch straight into the interview. Go for a few little pleasantries. Many people may have good stories to tell but are initially wary of notebooks and tape recorders. This is where small talk comes in handy. These minutes can be used to arrange your tape recorder, pen and notepad. Place the tape recorder closer to the subject than yourself, away from traffic, cappuccino machines, phones and so on. You don't need a cone of silence but a little peace and quiet helps.

The interview proper

The basis of an interview is usually common ground: the person has material which you need for your story. Remember that you are the guest. This does not mean you have to be timid and pliant. It's more a matter of recognising the nature of the relationship between yourself and the interviewee. Ask your questions politely, and make them part of the conversation.

You're fishing and hoping for answers that will eventually be part of the story you're writing. So you need to be alert to answers that could lead to further information. Listen also for answers that have gone long past the point. Look out for answers that don't even get to the point! Is the person speaking too generally, avoiding specifics? Is the person hedging around the question? Is the person rambling off the point? Be prepared to ad-lib your questions, moving away from the set list you've prepared. (The better prepared you are, the better you can cope with spontaneous situations and the more flexible you can be.)

Dumb questions, not stupid questions

If an answer confuses you, then backtrack a little and ask the person to answer the question again. You're looking for more material, not muddled material. Don't be afraid to show some lack of understanding. After all, if you're interviewing an expert, that person is supposed to know more than you. Ask 'dumb' questions if you have to. Ask the person to explain complex topics in a straightforward way.

Taking notes

Don't trust the tape recorder, no matter how many times you've checked the batteries. Take notes. Write key words and phrases, as well as points about the person's manner, dress and body language. However, be aware that taking too many notes can be self-defeating: you can lose eye-contact and momentum.

Thinking on three levels

This comes with experience. At the one time you could be doing three things: taking notes of what the subject has just said; listening to what the subject is currently saying; and preparing to ask your next question.

Listening well requires attention to detail, not just hearing words. Listening for nuances, good quotes, inflections and anecdotes that may be expanded, and eliminate questions that have already been answered. In normal conversations we cut in on one another, talk over each other, finish one another's sentences. In an interview you are listening more intently, and your interviewee should be the one doing most of the talking.

Pauses, silences and interruptions

Pauses are part and parcel of everyday conversation. We stop to ponder something for a few seconds and then we resume talking. The same applies to interviews. Don't try fill up a pause—give the interviewee time to answer your question.

Silence—a long pause—can be a problem if the interviewee is dodging rather than contemplating answers. You may have asked the person something they have not previously thought about, so silence is understandable. The interviewee is probably choosing words carefully, looking for the best way to express an answer.

There can also be interruptions. Use these to your advantage. If the interviewee is on the phone for a few minutes it gives you time to collect your thoughts, and to quickly scan—and review—your questions. A few interruptions can be handy. Too many, though, can be a hindrance.

Reliable equipment

Take spare batteries and cassettes for your tape recorder, extra biros and paper.

The last few minutes

Always end with an invitation to the interviewee to cover any topics not already covered. Try a little small talk as you leave: this can be very helpful because the subject, in a more relaxed mood, might be a bit more open. Don't stop listening just because you're packing up and saying goodbye.

After the interview

While the interview is fresh in your mind sit and make notes. Check that the tape recorder has worked and then relax. Let it all simmer until you come back to your desk.

Janet Hawley is regarded as one of Australia's finest profile writers. She has won three Walkley Awards for outstanding journalism, including the Gold Walkley in 1990. Encounters with Australian Artists, *the collection of her expanded profiles from* Good Weekend *magazine, was published in 1993. Here she gives some pointers about interviewing.*

You must have a genuine curiosity about the person or subject you're writing about. The person will then sense that you want to know things, that you want to listen and understand. Never lose that curiosity.

I start by doing as much research as I can. Then I put that research aside, and start out for a fresh look. The research, the preparation, gives you confidence. The more homework you've done, the more you've earned the right to interview that person. There's nothing worse than asking well-known people kindergarten questions. The interviewee will be bored, or insulted.

For my stories I will interview a person two or three times in different places and circumstances. All the time I'm developing trust and rapport. This can be hard for a young writer, who has yet to develop a reputation, and may not yet have lived through enough varied life experiences to gain crucial empathies. One of the most important elements of this trust is when people tell you things off the record. You must, must respect anything said off the record. You then show that you can be trusted with emotional and delicate issues.

Some people I've interviewed have exposed their innermost thoughts and soul. They are pleased to have a long and reflective talk. They may well tell me too much and I'll often self-censor on the person's behalf, because even though they haven't said 'this is off the record', you know they would want certain private things to remain private, and they would feel betrayed if you don't handle the conversation sensitively.

> I do huge amounts of taping for my stories. Then I play the tapes back, often several times. I listen to them when I'm gardening, or doing housework. Or driving back from the interview. I like to relive the person's words, moods and reactions. It helps me size up the character.
>
> I transcribe the parts of the tape that I need. Having played the tapes so much I can sometimes almost write from memory. I listen very carefully when I'm transcribing. There are subtleties you can pick up from the tape which you couldn't get just from notes . . .
>
> I do not let people I'm writing about see the story before it's published. If a person agrees to an interview then they are agreeing to trust you to do it well. It's like sitting for a portrait—you can't expect to grab the brush and make your own changes. The exceptions are when I'm writing especially technical stories, about medical, scientific or legal issues. Then I'm worried about making mistakes. So I check facts and direct quotes, and may ask an expert to read the story.

Transcribing

Transcribing—writing down the words of the interview—is crucial in terms of quoting accurately and capturing the subject's tone of voice and general attitude. It also forces you to listen to yourself as interviewer and evaluate your interviewing skills.

During the process of transcribing is when you confirm your hunches about which parts of the interview will be used as direct quotes, which will be retold in indirect quotes and which parts to ignore.

It is a time-consuming task but at the end you can rest assured you've covered everything. And you can always ring the subject back if you need to check things. With experience you develop a form of personal shorthand (or real shorthand) that shortcuts the tedium of transcribing. With further experience you learn not to transcribe each and every word, but only those parts you will use.

Here is an extract of a transcript of an interview with a musician, Gerry Hale:

> So we got started out as a very traditional American style of thing. We were playing standard bluegrass repertoire with a few of those older Pommy pop songs that I had picked up along the way and then I just started to get more curious about . . . I had worked in Melbourne for a few years and I had worked with a few great songwriters and I was looking at the material that was here and then just started slotting some of the songs into the set and thought it was working quite nicely.

In the published article, the quote appeared as:

> We started out as a very traditional American style of thing. We were playing standard bluegrass repertoire with a few of those older Pommy pop songs—The Who, The Kinks—that I had picked up along the way and then I just started to get more curious about Australian music.

This simple example shows a small degree of rewording of the original transcript. It tightens the text without taking away the rhythms or the meaning of the original quote. The interviewer has also rung back the interviewee and asked for more details about 'those older Pommy pop songs'.

Phone interviews

These are standard in the day-to-day world of news reporting. Phone-interviewing requires almost immediate rapport. Yes, you can still have small talk at the start—and the end—but there's no coffee to wait for or business phone calls to interrupt. Nor is there any body language or scene setting. You've just got to be a little bit sharper, be certain that your notes make sense, or buy a device that records telephone conversations.

In her book, *Reporting in Australia* (Macmillan Education Australia, Melbourne 1996, p. 95), Sally A. White notes that:

> Some interviewees prefer the anonymity of the phone and are far more forthcoming than they would be in person. And a few journalists prefer using the phone. They know that people find it easy not to open a door but hard to resist answering a phone . . . Start with a smile, even though the interviewee can't see it. The smile comes through in the voice. Try to pitch your voice reasonably low and speak relatively slowly. Remember during a long answer to indicate your continued attentiveness with the occasional 'mm'.

On-line and e-mail interviews

These are handy for collecting information, but otherwise are quite static. There's no chance to pick up on body language, tone of voice, setting, atmosphere and so on. They cannot replace the immediacy and intimacy of face-to-face interviews.

The reluctant interviewee

Despite Andy Warhol's claim that everybody will get their fifteen minutes of fame, there are some people who just do not wish to talk to the media. As a writer, you are caught between respecting their wishes and wanting to write a good story. You need, then, gentle powers of persuasion. You need to be able to justify the interview, to show why it's important the person is interviewed.

You may have to compromise: show your interviewee the questions in advance, perhaps, or offer to check facts and quotes with them after the feature is written.

But some people just will not be interviewed. Jack Denham, the trainer of the champion racehorse Might and Power, flatly refused to speak to the media after his horse won the 1997 Melbourne Cup. Racing writers were strongly divided in their opinion on his attitude.

Vetting the story

The interviewee may request to see your article before it's published. You need to use discretion here. Is the person 'media shy' or 'media smart'? With the former, it's an understandable response: the person may be wary of being misquoted or of being poorly presented on the page. The 'media smart' person, however, may be trying to manipulate the story, hoping to rewrite parts of it. Either way, offer to check facts and, perhaps, read some quotes over the phone, but that's all. Any more than that and you may find your article being extensively rewritten from a biased point of view. Exceptions to this advice occur when you are writing a particularly technical story or when you are doing an as-told-to article, in which the entire article is in the words of the interviewee.

Enjoying the interview

There can be many variables in an interview but if you are well prepared and keen to listen then you are on the way to enjoying one of the most stimulating aspects of feature writing. Generally, if you treat your interviewee with respect and show your interest in their story, you will be rewarded with good material.

Summary

- Interviews require solid preparation and sound listening
- Arrange questions in an order that will elicit facts, quotes and anecdotes
- Remember closed and open questions

- Don't be afraid to ask 'dumb' questions
- Choose a venue that is comfortable for the interviewee
- Be early
- Small talk can be very handy
- Be prepared to ad-lib, to move away from set questions
- Tape record and take notes
- Interruptions can be useful
- Think on three levels: listening, taking notes, preparing your next question
- Transcribe carefully
- Enjoy yourself

Exercises

1. Tape five minutes of a radio or television interview. Summarise what you learnt about the interviewee.

2. Listen (or watch) the tape again. What skills does the interviewer demonstrate?

3. Transcribe the tape word for word.

4. Which sentences or phrases from the transcription would you include if the story were to be published as an article?

5. Do vox pops with classmates and colleagues. A vox pop is asking several people two or three simple questions about the one topic. For example: Do you want a republic? (Why/Why not?) Who should be the head of state? How should that person be elected?

6. Write up the vox pop, then check whether you've quoted people accurately.

7. Interview a classmate or colleague for five minutes about a significant day in their life. Compile a list of closed and open questions that will help you collect facts, quotes and anecdotes. Tape record, and also take down notes. Pay

attention to body language, appearance, and, of course, the words.

8. Transcribe the interview.

9. Select which parts you would use as direct quotes in an article and which parts you would paraphrase.

eight Writing skills

> *When you're writing all the time, and reading all the time, you analyse what other people have written to see what they did and how they did it . . . I think my writing gets better all the time.*
>
> Dr Kimberley Ivory, freelance journalist and medical editor
> *That's Life* magazine

This chapter may seem to be all about rules. But the great thing about writing and rewriting regularly is that, after a while, you absorb the rules. If you write often enough, and revise often enough, most of the points we cover in this chapter will become second nature to you (if they aren't already).

Write well

What is a well-written piece? It's one that conveys exactly what you want to say to your reader. Good writing isn't about hiding behind big words which you may have done in essays at school or uni. Waffle or padding in a feature article sticks out a mile.

You are aiming for clarity and focus. But first you have to know what it is you are trying to say. If you don't understand or are confused about the points you are trying to make, then how will your reader understand you? That's why your early free-written draft is so important. In it you are working out what it is you are trying to say. The editing comes later.

Good writing is about interacting with your reader. It has all the good qualities of speech (with the ums and ahs cut out), and is personal and direct.

Writing well means writing clear, concise sentences and arranging facts logically in such a way that your reader knows where you are going and can follow you clearly all the way there. This chapter looks at some essentials for good non-fiction writing.

Keep your reader in mind

Whether you're writing for computer programmers, tree surgeons, social workers or the general public, the most important thing to bear in mind is your reader.

Picture your readers. Who are they? What do they already know about your topic? What words do they use in talking about it? Answers to these questions will guide your content and choice of words in the finished article.

For example, an article on asthma-free travel could be aimed at asthmatics reading the daily paper or at readers of *Australian Doctor* magazine. For the layperson you'd provide handy tips and explain each new term in a way that doesn't assume expert knowledge. With your medical audience, you would not have to explain what a 'ventilation pack' includes and you would use more technical language to describe irritants and symptoms. Tailoring your material to your audience is the trademark of the professional writer.

Writing with your reader in mind means leaving your ego at the front door. This may be difficult if you are tempted to use a feature article to showcase your talent with adjectives, but you have to remember you are writing for someone other than yourself.

First, words

What keeps your reader reading? Language that is easy to understand, vivid, to the point, simple, fresh and interesting. A successful article is one in which the reader gets so absorbed that they don't notice the writing. It flows smoothly and seamlessly from start to finish, and the reader is pulled effortlessly to the conclusion. That's the ideal.

In reality, there are many snags on which a reader (and a writer) can get caught. Examples of common snags are: unclear or poorly phrased sentences, long-winded sentences, and convoluted words that obscure meaning. What will turn your reader off is language that is complex, repetitive, abstract, archaic, academic, complicated, tiring, pretentious and above all, boring. If your reader has to struggle to work out what you mean, they'll get frustrated or bored or both, and give up.

Choose words that convey your meaning simply and clearly

Your objective isn't to impress your reader with your language skills, or the amount of research you've done. Your objective is for the reader to read one paragraph, and then the next and the next, all the way to the end.

Be concise

You are writing to fill a space, and the more economically you write, the better. Each word you use has to earn its place in your story.

Being concise means using as few words as possible to say what you mean, turning wordy sentences into short ones without losing information. Being concise means using *house* instead of *dwelling*, *hurry* instead of *expedite*, *count* instead of *enumerate*. Apply the same rule to phrases:

Phrase		Word
as a consequence of	*becomes*	because
at the present time	*becomes*	now
in excess of	*becomes*	more
with the exception of	*becomes*	except

Avoid pompous words

Often beginner writers add words in their writing that they think will impress their reader by making the writer sound more educated, or more important. Take the case of Peter. He'd left school at fifteen and joined the public service. He worked his way up over the years from clerical assistant to head of department. There he was, seventeen years after joining, head of a department full of people with postgraduate university degrees. Peter was a direct and colloquial speaker. He was an avid punter and often used racing analogies in his speech as a way of making a point. When he hadn't made up his mind about which applicant would get a job, he said he was 'still studying the form'. When he decided to go ahead with a risky but potentially exciting new project he'd tell staff he'd decided to 'take a punt'. But when it came to putting pen to paper, his confidence evaporated. His memos to staff were dull, wordy and full of jargon.

Sometimes new or nervous writers add words as a shield, believing they can hide behind big words because they are not sure what it is they are trying to say. Look at these examples:

> We must action a needs assessment of the downturn in
> entrance applications for the course.
> *means*
> We need to find out why no one is applying for the course.

Prune empty words

Get rid of unnecessary words. Prune. Be ruthless. These words are the dead wood in your writing. They serve no useful purpose. They are often words that repeat what you have already said. They are not only not missed when they're cut, but their absence makes a big improvement to your writing. It will be clearer and sharper. Are the italicised phrases in the following sentences necessary?

> Our new fitness program includes *the added feature of* water aerobics.
>
> The knitting was *of an* inferior *quality*.
>
> The police relied on *the element of* surprise to capture the thief.

Avoid tautologies

Don't use two words to express the same idea. In the following examples, the italicised words are unnecessary:

> The two companies merged *together*.
> The parachutist plummeted *down*.

Use concrete words

Being concrete means choosing words that are specific rather than vague. This way you create a picture in the reader's mind of what it is you are talking about. Being detailed in your descriptions forces you to be more observant. Compare the following pairs of sentences.

1. Joe has had lots of jobs in the past.
2. Joe has had 63 jobs in the last ten years.

1. The food in the restaurant was expensive.
2. The two-course meal cost the couple $250.

1. As I was interviewing the police psychologist, she was called away to another emergency.
2. As I was interviewing the police psychologist, she was called away to talk to a man who was threatening to jump off the roof of a twenty-storey building.

Keep your writing lively

Avoid over-used phrases or clichés, fashionable words, officialese or jargon that is meaningless to your reader. Don't waste tired old words and phrases on a fresh and interesting idea. Examples of stale expressions include: *no stone unturned*, *by the same token*, *grind to a halt*, *a tower of strength*, *as white as a sheet*.

Choose strong nouns and verbs

Often we use adverbs and adjectives to support weak verbs or nouns. Use strong nouns and verbs instead. This will make your writing more colourful and concise. In the following example adverbs (in italics) are being used to describe the way a woman walked.

She walked *wearily* and *laboriously* up the hill.

By choosing a stronger verb than walked, the sentence tells us more in fewer words.

She trudged up the hill.

Adjectives can be used in the same way to prop up a weak noun.

A *long white* car slowed to a halt outside the restaurant.

A limousine slowed to a halt outside the restaurant.

A *large group of* women *called out loudly* to *the man in uniform who guarded* the doors of the department store.

At 9 am the doors opened and the women *pushed hurriedly* inside. The sale *had commenced*.

One thousand women yelled at the security guard inside the department store until the doors opened at 9 am and they spilled inside. The sale was on.

In all these examples, the use of a stronger noun or verb instead of an adjective or adverb gives you much better value. Strong nouns and verbs convey more detailed information in fewer words.

Use active voice

Look at the following sentence.

>The article   was edited by him.
>subject

It's written in the passive voice which results in wordier sentences and weak verbs. Passive-voice sentences are those where the subject of the sentence is not acting but being acted on. In other words, they contain a subject that is the receiver of an action.

>He   edited the article.
>subject

The rewritten version is in the active voice. In active-voice sentences, the subject is the 'doer' or agent of an action. The active-voice version delivers the information contained in it more quickly. We know immediately who edited what. The passive-voice version of the sentence is longer than the active.

Generally, it is best to write in the active voice. Active-voice sentences are shorter and stronger and convey more information than passive-voice sentences.

Changing passive to active voice

Start by looking for the verb in the following passive-voice sentence.

The tree was *demolished* by the truck.

What did the demolishing? This is the agent of the action. Put the thing or person *doing* the demolishing at the beginning of the sentence.

The truck demolished what?

Now for the receiver of the action. What was demolished?

The truck demolished *the tree*.

Now it's in active voice. Sometimes passive-voice sentences lack an agent. For example,

Mr Smith was kicked.

We know Mr Smith was the receiver of the kick, but who did the kicking? To turn passive sentences like this into active-voice sentences, you have to identify the agent and insert it yourself. Active-voice sentences force you to identify who did the action.

The horse kicked Mr Smith.

Passive-voice sentences are a tradition of scientific and official writing where the writer wants to appear impersonal and objective by absenting him- or herself from the sentence.

The effect of alcohol on decision-making skills of adult rats was studied. (Passive voice)

I studied the effect of alcohol on adult rats' decision making. (Active voice)

You can see now why active voice is preferred in news and feature writing—it is direct, simple and informal. It forces you to identify who-did-what in the most economical and liveliest way.

When to use passive voice

Use the passive voice when it is the process or what was done that you want to emphasise. For example:

> The burglar was last seen in Martin Plaza.

What you are emphasising is the fact that the burglar was spotted, and it doesn't matter by whom. Use the passive voice when you want to conceal information or delay the introduction of information to the reader, for example for humour:

> The picnic was interrupted—by a herd of elephants.

Know the difference between active and passive voice, and the effect each has on the reader. Then you can choose which one to use for the best result.

Write for rhythm and meaning

Using parallel patterns makes your writing flow smoothly and helps the reader make connections between elements of the piece.

Version 1
Activities included in the package are swimming and camping, and snorkel sets are also available.

The final phrase in version 1 of this sentence has a jarring effect, and will pull your reader up in the course of reading it. Compare it to the rewritten version.

Version 2
Activities included in the package are swimming, camping and snorkelling.

Version 2 has an easy rhythm and the meaning is clearer. Use parallel construction within sentences, paragraphs and lists.

Version 1
Ways to reduce stress
Take deep breaths.
Good friends can help if you talk about your stress.
Brisk walking can relieve the build-up of tension.
Play your favourite music.
Soaking in a hot tub relaxes tense muscles.
If you make a list of what you need to get done, you'll feel more in control.
Ask people to help you.
When you do something that you've got on your list, reward yourself.

Version 2
Ways to reduce stress
Practise deep breathing.
Talk to a good friend about what's worrying you.
Take a brisk walk to relieve tension.
Play your favourite music.
Soak in a hot tub.
Make a list of all things that you have to do.
Ask people to help you.
Reward yourself each time you complete something on your list.

Version 2 has been rewritten so that each point in the list begins with a verb. Setting up a pattern like this helps your reader anticipate what will follow. It is easier to read, and easier to understand.

Dr Kimberley Ivory's first articles appeared in Australian Family Physician *and* Medical Observer *in 1992. In 1994, she joined* That's Life *magazine as medical editor. She also writes for a number of other publications. Her specialities are health, travel and lifestyle.*

There are lots of things I didn't know when I started because I didn't have a journalistic background. I had to wing it a bit, but I also read a lot about what I was doing.

I learnt about writing by reading lots of books about journalistic writing. The editor at *Medical Observer* at the time was also very helpful to me. She taught me a lot about the process. I also subscribed to magazines, joined the Australian Medical Writers Association and learnt more about the business. You can't be precious. No matter how good you think it is, if it doesn't meet the editor's needs, they won't publish it.

I understand much more now about what's required in writing than I did when I started—the difference between news, features, opinion pieces and how not to editorialise. I learned to write in different styles for different audiences. For example, in *Medical Observer* I can use more complex language that includes accepted jargon because it's for a medical audience. For *That's Life* I have to write for a lower reading age; when I'm tired, stressed or in a hurry I find I have to make a conscious effort to write simply, otherwise I lapse into jargon.

I had to unlearn things that aren't acceptable in journalism. Referral letters between doctors use phrases like 'herewith' and are written in passive voice. Once I started writing regularly for magazines I could no longer write in that style. Now I find it cumbersome and clumsy.

I had to learn to write short sentences, to explain medical terms in simple words, to sum up an idea in two sentences rather than two pages. I've had to reduce a journal article to a paragraph. When I'm doing this I ask myself what my readers are likely to ask. 'What's in this for me? How's it going to affect my life?'

Summary

- Keep your reader in mind
- Be concise
- Avoid pompous words
- Prune empty words
- Avoid tautologies
- Use concrete words
- Choose strong nouns and verbs
- Use active voice
- Write for rhythm and meaning

Exercises

1. Replace these long words and phrases with a shorter word which says the same thing.

    incinerate
    desire
    locality
    purchase
    reside
    provided that
    prior to
    gave permission to

2. Rewrite the following sentences in simple and direct style.

    Pedestrians are requested to refrain from conversation with the lollipop man during working hours.

    I was desirous that she accompany me to the ball.

Jane informed her father that she had had a fine imposed on her car for incorrect parking.

3. Weed out unnecessary words in these sentences.

   The temple is the most unique of its kind.

   It was clear the bottle was quite empty.

   The burglar broke into the house in broad daylight.

   They paired off in twos to decorate the house for the party.

   It is required that jurors arrive punctually and on time.

4. Replace the abstract words or phrases in the following sentences with more concrete ones.

   Steven and Bill sat around the coffee table, playing a game.

   He parked the vehicle.

   She used a tool and fixed the appliance.

5. With a partner or a group, think of as many clichés as you can.

6. Which of the following sentences are in active and which are in passive voice?

   A group of fans chased the soccer coach.

   Might and Power won the Melbourne Cup.

   A truck hit the car.

   The burglar was seen by the housekeeper.

   You are loved by me.

   Two thousand people signed the petition.

   She cooked a cheese souffle.

   Stress and coping skills were studied in a group of Quit counsellors.

Lack of space and lack of time for planning were identified as problems.

The nurse changed the sheets.

Drinking and cooking water was obtained by channelling run-off from the roof into a rainwater tank.

7. Rewrite the passive voice sentences into active voice.

8. Rewrite the original active voice sentences into passive voice.

9. Rewrite the following to improve rhythm and meaning.

    The company's recreation centre is interested in higher membership, lower overheads and wants customers to reach their goals.

    Her meticulous grooming, calm manner and being forthright impressed the members of the panel.

    Winter camping checklist. In addition to the tent, take:
    - waterproof torch
    - raincoat, with hood
    - for extra warmth, down-filled sleeping bags are best for cold nights
    - stove (make sure it's portable)
    - sleeping on the floor of a tent is cold. Bring an inflatable mattress and foot pump
    - axe (a sturdy one)

10. Keep a scrapbook or journal of long, wordy or generally poorly expressed sentences. Rewrite them using a simple and direct style.

11. Clip an article from a specialist journal written for a professional audience. Rewrite it for a lay audience.

Answers to exercises

1. burn
   want
   place
   buy
   live
   if
   before
   allowed

2. Please don't talk to the lollipop man while he's working.

   I wanted her to come with me to the ball.

   Jane told her father that she had been given a parking fine.

3. The temple is unique.

   It was clear the bottle was empty.

   The burglar broke into the house in daylight.

   They paired off to decorate the house for the party.

   It is required that jurors arrive punctually.

4. Steven and Bill sat around the coffee table, playing Scrabble/chess/dominoes etc.

   He parked the car/truck/bus.

   She used a screwdriver/hammer and fixed the washing machine/blender/hairdryer.

6. A group of fans chased the soccer coach. Active

   Might and Power won the Melbourne Cup. Active

   A truck hit the car. Active

   The burglar was seen by the housekeeper. Passive

You are loved by me. Passive

Two thousand people signed the petition. Active

She cooked a cheese souffle. Active

Stress and coping skills were studied in a group of Quit counsellors. Passive

Lack of space and lack of time for planning were identified as problems. Passive

The nurse changed the sheets. Active

Drinking and cooking water was obtained by channelling run-off from the roof into a rainwater tank. Passive

7. The housekeeper saw the burglar.

   I love you.

   The researchers studied stress and coping skills in a group of Quit counsellors.

   The consultant identified the problems as lack of space and lack of time for planning.

   The settlers obtained drinking and cooking water by channelling run-off from the roof into a rainwater tank.

8. The soccer coach was chased by a group of fans.

   The Melbourne Cup was won by Might and Power.

   The car was hit by a truck.

   The petition was signed by 2000 people.

   A cheese souffle was cooked by her.

   The sheets were changed by the nurse.

9. The company's recreation centre is interested in higher

membership, lower overheads and improved customer satisfaction.

Her meticulous grooming, calm manner and forthright opinions impressed the members of the interview panel.

Winter camping checklist. In addition to the tent, take:
- waterproof torch
- hooded raincoat
- down-filled sleeping bags
- portable stove
- inflatable mattress and foot pump
- sturdy axe

nine Drafting and crafting

I read with a mental red pen. I edit everything I read. This is now your job—mentally editing everything you read—a letter in your mailbox, a story in your local paper, a memo from your boss, a circular from your local MP. Look at all of them and think about how you'd improve them.

Maree Curtis, senior features writer, *Age*

Writing is an art, yes, but it's also a profession. Writers of good non-fiction do not just wait for inspiration. Writing takes practice, it takes discipline and it takes time. Like all professional writers, you will have to work through several drafts.

In the process of drafting and crafting your feature article you will clarify your thoughts on the topic, hone your angle and experience a point where all the seemingly unconnected pieces fall into a pattern. But before you get to that stage, you have to start at the beginning. Before you can start editing and shaping your piece, you need to have written a first draft.

Write a draft

Pick up your piles of notes (those from books, or journals, or interviews that you've done), put them in a folder and put the folder in a drawer. Now make a draft of the story using what sticks in your mind. Don't worry if you can't think of anything to start with, things will occur to you once you start writing. You may run out of steam after three or four paragraphs but the story will have been forming in your mind without you noticing.

Write first, edit later

We can't emphasise this point enough. Do not edit as you go. If necessary, write with the screen of your computer turned off or with carbon paper and an empty pen. Think aloud on paper first—with ramblings, half thoughts, vivid images and flashes of insight. Get the big picture down first, focus on detail later.

Your purpose is not to get up from your desk at this stage with a publishable story in your hands. Your purpose is to work out your thinking on the topic and, in order to do that, you have to be able to sit down and let the words flow on paper. If it helps, ignore punctuation, grammar and spelling. This draft is for you, no one else. It isn't meant to be perfect. Perfection comes later.

Stopping to rewrite at first-draft stage is like constantly being interrupted while you're trying to speak. Don't interrupt yourself. Don't stop to worry over detail. Write without stopping, get your thoughts down on paper, follow hunches, think aloud, try to express on paper what it is that excites you or intrigues you about this topic. Spill everything out at one sitting. Writing an uninhibited (and completely unedited) first draft can feel messy and chaotic, but writing an article is very much a process of writing your way towards meaning.

Read your research notes

Once you've got your draft down on paper, put it away for a few hours or days. Get your folder of notes out of the drawer. Read quickly through all the notes you've made on this topic. Skim. As you go, make notes on what conclusions you can come to from your material. Use headings or dot points and make a note of what will go in each. Note any endings that jump out at you.

Revisit your angle/theme

Rewrite your angle or theme in one or two sentences. Here you are refining what it is you are going to say in your story.

Don't be surprised if your angle now is different from when you started. Before, your angle was a hunch, an idea. Now you've read the evidence you've gathered, you have to look at that angle again. For example, the original angle for a story on women jockeys may have been the reasons why the number of women jockeys is increasing in your state.

But your research may have uncovered the fact that the number of women jockeys hasn't increased in recent years, and in fact fewer women are riding. Your article then becomes an exploration of why it is still such a male-dominated occupation.

Remember, if your angle was specific enough and you did your research thoroughly, this part should be relatively easy. Much of the struggle and frustration that can occur at this stage can be a result of not having asked the right questions at the research stage or having a vague and unfocussed angle in the first place.

Nevertheless, you can also expect to feel overwhelmed, even disorganised at this stage. Like tidying a messy desk, you'll be engaged in sifting, sorting, putting notes into piles, and categorising things as either to be used or to be filed away for another story.

Structure your story

Now you have a first draft, notes on what your research tells you and a sentence or two on what your story is about. This material is the equivalent of a pile of building blocks that you have to put together into a shape that gives meaning to the story. That shape may already be obvious to you. You may also find that the structure of the story is there in your first draft, that it emerged as you wrote.

Let's say you're doing an article on fear of public speaking. You've got a lot of factual information, quotes from experts you've spoken to, notes on a course you attended on overcoming fear of public speaking, and a pile of examples or case studies of people with a fear of public speaking. Now think of a way of organising these pieces logically for your reader.

Your building blocks might go like this: size of the problem, how prevalent it is, examples of people who suffer from it and solutions. A story on the restoration of your local theatre may be made up of the following building blocks: the theatre when it was built last century, the theatre now and plans for it in the future. Your story on a guided tour of a goldmine may have a chronological shape, following the tour as it happened in time so that the shape of your story is the beginning of the tour, the middle and the end. However you identify the chunks or building blocks of your story, remember to keep each 'chunk' together in your story. Otherwise the story can jump around all over the place and confuse your reader.

Of course, there are always exceptions. You can successfully weave history throughout a feature article as a linking device. And you should avoid overloading your reader with statistics. Space statistical information through the story. Use numbers to support the development of your theme rather than throwing them all in one or two adjoining paragraphs.

Make your numbers work for you. Simplify them or put

them in the form of a picture that a reader can visualise. For example, if 25 per cent of personal trainers' clients are schoolteachers, say one in four clients are schoolteachers. If you are using a large number, help the reader visualise it. Ninety slabs of beer becomes 'enough to fill a backyard swimming pool'.

Give each block of your story its allotted and logical amount of space. For example, in a story profiling three night shift workers, give each worker roughly equal space.

There's no one right way of ordering your material—the main test is whether or not it is logical and flows smoothly. Don't underestimate your readers—they will be quick to pick up any inconsistencies or obvious gaps.

Choose quotes

You may interview several people while researching an article but it won't be necessary to quote all of them. Most will provide you with information that is background. Choose to quote people who have a clear purpose in your story. Be careful not to clutter your story with minor characters.

Whether you use direct quotes (the person's exact words in quotation marks) or indirect speech (reported in the third person or paraphrased), make sure you are quoting accurately. Report the person's words as they were spoken if you are quoting directly. You can correct the grammar in a quote but, as when you are using indirect speech, make sure that you do not alter the meaning the speaker intended.

Generally, it's best to keep quotes from the same person in one place. In the theatre story, chunk the quotes from the heritage architect in one section, then move to the projectionist who's been there for 60 years. By keeping each person separate, you are allowing each speaker to make an impact on readers before they read about the next person.

Set high standards for the quotes you use. Don't use quotes to convey basic information. Quote the heritage architect talking about the first time he saw the inside of the wonderful old theatre, not talking about when the theatre was built or how many seats it has. Quote people directly when they express an opinion, when they reveal a strong feeling, or when they express themselves in a much better way than you could have. Quotes add people and variety to your story.

Make quotes flow

Introducing quotes into your story requires some preparation for your reader. Like bridges between paragraphs, the line or two that precedes a quote should help the reader anticipate what will follow. Often readers get snagged or pulled up by a quote that has been dropped into the middle of the story with a clunk. You are aiming to weave your quotes seamlessly throughout your story.

You can create links for your reader so that the quote flows logically and smoothly from the sentence before it. Here's an example from an interview with a woman horse trainer.

> Shelley believes the secret to being a good trainer is in doing a lot of homework. 'You've got to study the breed, you've got to be up on things all the time. I do a lot of listening to and reading of top trainers. The older trainers are just so knowledgeable, they've got a lifetime of experience all stored up.'

The word 'homework' links to the word 'study' in the first sentence of the quote to create a smooth transition and introduction to the words that are quoted. When the reader has been led to expect one thing and the quote fails to deliver, confusion results. Look at the next quote from a horse trainer.

> Joanne says there's a lot of satisfaction in watching a horse that's been trained make the grade. 'It's awful when they lose. Sometimes you feel like giving up.'

The reader expects that Joanne will talk about how it feels when a horse wins a race, instead, the quote begins with her words about how it feels when a horse loses. Effective links help readers to make the connection, they help readers see the logic between individual sentences and paragraphs.

Show, don't tell

Feature writers rely on their ability to paint pictures with words so that the reader is drawn in close to detail and gets a vivid sense of the story. Don't tell the reader what you want to convey, show them. Telling can be like an annoying voice-over in a movie. It distances the reader from the action.

Showing your reader means recording sensory detail—the sights, smells, sounds and feel of things to create a vivid image that the reader can experience.

He got sunburnt. (Telling)

His skin tingled and tightened as he lay in the heat of the sun. (Showing)

Marianna was bored. (Telling)

Marianna drummed her fingers on the tabletop, sighed, got up and walked around like a caged animal and then slumped back in the chair and sighed again. (Showing)

Things were tough for the Smeaton family. (Telling)

Mrs Smeaton's jumper was darned and worn. Every night Mrs Smeaton boiled potatoes for tea. The smaller children scavenged along the banks of the creek for wild fennel and on a lucky night Mr Smeaton brought home a rabbit. (Showing)

Look at the following example:

The Horseshoe Bend township was typical of a village in the 1920s. Located on a river, the town was a busy place employing many people and offering shopping, services and a social centre to the local community. (Telling)

Now compare it with this excerpt from a story by former student Yvonne Blake:

> Steam engines chug, the printing press clanks, horse harnesses jingle and the riverboat's paddles 'thwump thwump' the water as it approaches the wharf. Around the corner comes a clattering of hooves and a cloud of dust signals the arrival of the Cobb and Co. coach at the Post Office.
>
> Beads of sweat drip from the blacksmith's face as he beats and shapes the white-hot metal. Ladies compare laces in the haberdashery. From the music shop's pianola, popular tunes drift out onto the street.
>
> At noon, the stock and station agent and bank manager stroll over to the inn for a plate of cold meat. Outside the local garage, a proud owner takes delivery of the first motorised vehicle in the district, as the photographer records the moment for history.
>
> It's mid afternoon and the schoolhouse bell clangs. Children with ink-stained fingers grab bridles and race to the paddock beside the school where ponies have waited since morning to return their young riders to their outlying homes.
>
> As dusk settles, labourers converge on the Mechanics Institute Hall for some book learning and the town's leading businessmen gather at the Masonic Lodge Temple.
>
> On Saturday nights, the rafters of the bush hall shake as dancers pound the floor for the lancers and progressive barn dance. On Sunday mornings, the nearby inter-denominational church witnesses many of the same faces in sober, pious worship. (Showing)

The telling paragraph is a rather flat, summary piece of writing. The student's example, while longer, brings the township alive for the reader and reveals more about the town and its people.

Of course, there is a place for telling versus showing in feature writing, just as there is for passive and active voice. The point is to know the difference, and to choose which to use for maximum effect.

Draft and redraft

Crafting and shaping your story means writing a number of drafts. Each draft will get you closer to what it is you are trying to say.

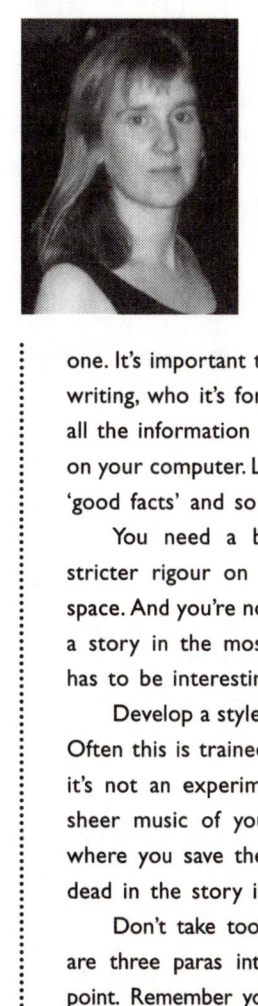

Michelle Griffin is a freelance feature writer and reviewer. She'll write about anything so long as there is money involved, but prefers to write about books, law, the Internet and 'lifestyle'. She got her start with a suburban newspaper, moved to a glossy feature magazine, and has been writing without a safety net since 1996.

Drafting and crafting can be an instinctive process but it can also be quite a conscious one. It's important to figure out first what kind of story it is you're writing, who it's for and how long it will be. Go through and put all the information you've gathered into piles on the floor or files on your computer. Label them 'good quotes', 'background', 'history', 'good facts' and so on.

You need a basic grip on grammar. Non-fiction demands stricter rigour on simple style than fiction. There's not enough space. And you're not writing for yourself. You are aiming to explain a story in the most interesting way possible. The first sentence has to be interesting enough to lead to the second and so on.

Develop a style. Write in active voice. Write simply and clearly. Often this is trained out of people who've been to university. And it's not an experimental piece. You can't charm people with the sheer music of your prose. Features are not like short stories where you save the punchline till the end . . . if someone drops dead in the story it's better to put it in the first paragraph.

Don't take too long to warm up to your topic. Some people are three paras into the story and they still haven't got to the point. Remember your reader is not interested in experts, they are interested in people. Don't have your story full of talking heads, keep it to two or three experts—and make sure they don't hog the space.

Another challenge is coming up with a satisfying shape—be aware that your story needs a particular theme or angle or shape to make it work. The old circular story, for example, where the last paragraph harks back to something in the first paragraph, is often effective.

The second draft is the time to rip out all of the bits that don't work—the jargon, the tendency to creep into a fact rather than stating it outright. You might start with 'It could be considered that . . .' Take it out. Get started with the thing you want to tell people.

Seek feedback

At the start of this book we said you need to develop a thick skin as a writer of feature articles. We also said that you shouldn't expect feedback from editors—they're generally too busy and it's not their role.

So how do you become a good critic of your own work?

Feedback from fellow writers

If you are part of a writing course then your fellow students and lecturers can provide you with feedback on your articles. If you aren't a member of a course but you want to get some assessment of your work, consider joining a writing group of like-minded people.

Writers' groups usually meet regularly for a specified amount of time. Members of the group bring along enough copies of their story for the rest of the group to read. The story is given out, read and then group members give the writer feedback. This process is called workshopping. Alternatively, in some writers' groups, the story is mailed out to group members so that the meeting time is taken up with discussion rather than reading. Groups can be as small as four, as large as twenty. Size doesn't matter as much as enthusiasm.

Your state writers' centre should have a list of writing groups that you can join. If there's nothing in your area, or if the ones that are in your area focus mainly on fiction or poetry, you have two options—set up one yourself or join an electronic writers' group through the Internet.

Set up a writers' group

To set up your group, advertise for members through word of mouth, your library, local newspapers, your state writer's centre or local bookshop. Meet somewhere neutral—a local library or community centre—at a time that suits everyone.

Spell out what you want

Spend the first meeting getting to know one another and discussing how you'd like the group to operate. This can involve issues such as how often to meet, what committment members should make in terms of writing and reading, and ground rules for giving and receiving feedback.

A good writers' group is one where people listen respectfully to one another, where feedback is offered without malice and in a spirit of helpfulness and enthusiasm, and where everyone in the group is committed to being a better writer. A good writers' group forces you to extend your skills as a writer. When they work well, they are exhilarating and you learn a lot.

By being exposed to the work of other people in the group as well as having your own work circulated and discussed you become a better reader, a better writer and a better editor of your own and other people's work.

You can practice writing to a deadline, you can do writing exercises in your group, you can swap gossip and ideas. You can share useful market information. You can support one another in the face of rejection and you can celebrate publication together.

In time, you may feel you've grown out of the need for a writers' group. That's fine. It suggests that the group has done its job and you are now able to look at your work quite objectively.

Commercial manuscript assessment services are available for a fee—contact your state writers' centre for details.

Freelance writer Rhonda Whitton believes it is important to be objective about your writing.

> Very early in your career, you will need to develop the ability to critique your work. By critiquing I mean that you need to be able to write a piece, then sit back and review it from the reader's perspective rather than from your own (sometimes self-indulgent) perspective.
>
> However, if you believe you need a mentor to critically review and appraise your work, don't show it to your mother or a friend who writes fiction. Chances are they will merely say 'It's wonderful'. You are better off to develop a relationship with someone who has a good working knowledge of the markets and who has the expertise to really critique your work.
>
> Personally, I believe you are best, very early in your career, to develop these skills and learn about being a freelance writer by reading the works of others and becoming familiar with your target publications. It's all part of serving an apprenticeship.

Summary

Drafting and crafting

- Write first, edit later
- Read your research notes

- Revisit your angle/theme
- Structure your story
- Choose quotes
- Make quotes flow
- Show, don't tell
- Expect to write a number of drafts

Getting feedback

Successful writers' groups:

- help you improve your writing
- help you identify your strengths
- have clear criteria for how to judge feature articles
- provide specific feedback
- help you develop a thick skin
- teach you how to give and receive constructive feedback
- extend your skills as a writer
- share useful market information
- help you achieve your goals

Exercises

Drafting and crafting

1. Turn off the screen or monitor of your computer. If you don't have a separate switch to do this, drape a scarf or something over the screen so that you can't see it. Write for fifteen minutes without stopping. Make this the first draft of your feature article. Forget grammar, spelling and punctuation at this stage. If you prefer to handwrite, do this exercise with a piece of carbon paper placed between two sheets of lined paper. Now start writing on the top sheet with a pen that doesn't work. Your words won't show on the piece of paper you're writing on, but they will appear on the page underneath the carbon.

122 WRITE TO PUBLISH

> The aim of this exercise is to free you up for your early drafts, to tap your creativity and to help you become more spontaneous. When you have finished, congratulate yourself and put the piece away for a day.

2. Look at three stories in appendix 1 and identify techniques the writer used to make them flow, including links between paragraphs, setting up quotes and any other transitional devices.

3. Using a transcript of an interview you did in chapter 7, go through and highlight the quotes you'd use and write down why you would use them.

4. Choose five quotes from your transcript and set them up so that they flow from one to another.

5. Jot down five points that the interviewee makes in your own words. Now choose a quote to support each point.

6. Rewrite the following 'telling' sentences so that they show the reader what you mean. Remember to concentrate on sensory detail.

   > Ipswich is a multicultural town.
   >
   > The winery is located in delightful surroundings.
   >
   > The opera singer behaved like a brat.
   >
   > Smith Street is attracting fashionable young people to its shops, but surrounding streets are full of poverty.
   >
   > Locals showed their anger at council plans to open a tip next to the playground.

7. Now go back to the draft you wrote in exercise 1. Make any changes you think you need to help the story flow.

8. Keep a timesheet for your story from the first draft onwards. Keep a record of how much time you spend

drafting and redrafting it. Compare this initial timesheet to ones you keep for subsequent stories. Watch how you become more efficient in the drafting process.

Getting feedback

Answer these questions about your current or ideal writers' group.

1. List the explicit rules of your group.
2. List the implicit rules that operate in your group.
3. Make a list of the goals of individual members of your group.
4. Write an advertisement for your ideal feedback partner.
5. Invite a published feature writer to come along and talk to your group about how and when they started writing features.
6. Compare the two articles on procrastination in appendix 1. One is written for the pages of a large metropolitan daily, the other for a women's magazine. Discuss how the articles are tailored for the two publications.
7. Find a feature published on the same topic in a newspaper and in a magazine. Read them both and apply your workshopping guidelines to them.
8. Write a first-person account about the first time you had something workshopped or the first time you attended a writers' group.

ten The top and the tail of the story

Often the first three to five paragraphs of an unpublished story are written in a very self-conscious way. It takes the writer a while to get to the meat of the story. This is what I call the 'throat-clearing syndrome'.

Pat Hayes, editor, *On the Road*

I develop a story as long as it has momentum. I don't consciously write a conclusion.

Kate Arnold, journalist

The top of the story may be all that editors and readers read. Editors can instinctively pick a good story quickly. They don't have the time, or the interest, to read every word of every article that comes across their desks. Most readers prefer to browse before reading a complete story and need a strong opening to be drawn past the pictures and advertisements, and into your story. It doesn't take long to turn the page and move onto another article, another topic.

How, then, to write the start of the story? You have at your disposal all that you've gathered in research: facts, figures, quotes, little stories, observations, questions, ruminations, phrases and descriptions. You may also have, either on paper or floating about in your mind, song lyrics, colloquial phrases, names of movies, lines from poems or childhood memories.

Any of these could form the basis of the title (or headline), the precede (a summary that often follows the title) and the lead (the opening paragraphs). You must try to find short phrases for titles, a sentence or two for precedes and effective opening lines for the lead. It is a rare, and valuable, writer who can put all these elements together. Don't worry. Many writers are only adept at one or two of these features of the top of the story.

The top of the story has to sparkle, draw readers in and make them want to read on. A poor beginning jeopardises the rest of your story, so be patient when working on this part of the article. Since editors or subeditors usually write the titles and precedes, regardless of how good yours may be, let's concentrate on leads first.

The lead

Your opening paragraph has to get the attention of your editor and reader. The type of article can dictate the length of a lead. A list or instructional article will have a very brief lead. A profile or news feature could have a longer lead. Here are some ideas for leads.

- Make a statement—and then justify it.
- Announce a fact—then follow it up with more detail.
- Use a famous name or title. The *X Files* spawned a plethora of leads, even if the articles weren't directly about the TV program or its stars.
- Describe a setting, beginning with a panoramic view and honing in on the subject, getting closer and closer with each short paragraph.
- Use a quote from an interview.
- Tell an anecdote.

- Create some mystery. Tease the reader with the start of an anecdote—and complete it further into the story.
- Quote some lines from a song, poem or novel.
- Shock—but make it work, don't just use it as a cheap device.
- Start at the middle or the end of a major incident of the story, then work your way back. This puts readers right into the thick of the action and has them wanting to know the answer to key questions: What happens next? Why did this happen? How did that happen? (Your story, of course, answers such questions.)
- Ask a question and then answer it, either immediately, or by the end of the story.

A good lead can also be the key to structuring the rest of the story. Or you may work the other way around: write the bulk of the article and then work out how it starts. That may sound like putting the cart before the horse but in creativity there are no hard and fast rules.

Good Weekend journalist Janet Hawley says this about leads:

> Those first . . . paragraphs are always difficult. I handwrite them, till I get the structure and rhythm right. Then I use my computer. Once I've got the start rolling, I'm on the way. It never gets easier to start a story.

Titles

There are many types of titles and most, though not quite all, have one thing in common: brevity. Titles can be as short as one word but not much longer than half a dozen. A long title is a novelty.

Here are a handful of titles from *HQ Magazine*, issue 60, September–October 1998.

- 'Sympathy for the devil'—best known as a song by The Rolling Stones, this is the title for a profile of satirist, comedian and TV host Paul McDermott.
- 'Once were cone heads'—this phrase plays on two movie titles, *Once Were Warriors* and *Cone Heads*. The story is a news feature on cannabis addiction.
- 'The bald & the beautiful'—a pun on the TV soapie *The Bold and the Beautiful*. The story is a humorous first-person anecdote about match-making a bald man with a beautiful woman.
- 'The name game'—three simple words, a simple rhyme. This feature is about pseudonyms.
- 'Magic beans'—a slightly cryptic title, short but not quite to the point. The article is a news feature about genetic engineering of crops.

The puns and the deliberate lifting of song and movie titles in the first three examples show that there's no copyright on titles. Depending on the topic, you can call an article 'Strictly ballroom', 'Muriel's wedding', 'Great expectations' or 'Of mice and men' . . .

It's great if you have a knack for titles but don't be disheartened if your witty wordplays and clever puns are changed. Here are some titles and what became of them when the stories were published:

- 'At the tip of the shovel'—a gardening anecdote about dead mice in the compost. The eventual title was 'Of mice, men and mortality'.
- 'The summer songs of Paul Kelly'—part-list, part-essay, this article was published as 'Under the sun in Kelly country'.
- 'The last service station'—an essay about changes to service stations became 'Progress means never having to say "fill 'er up."'.

Pat Hayes is editor and publisher of On the Road, *a national camping and caravanning magazine. His extensive journalism career includes stints with* The Horsham Times, Australian Motor Sports *and* Automobiles, The Times (London), *the* Age, Your Garden *and* Home Beautiful.

Here, Pat gives some tips on beginnings of stories.

Often the first three to five paragraphs of an unpublished story are written in a very self-conscious way. It takes the writer a while to get to the meat of the story. This is what I call the 'throat-clearing syndrome'. The writer is either telling us too much of what we're about to read, or is being pompous about their role in the story. I see quite experienced writers still doing this. But if you discard those first three to five paragraphs, all of a sudden the story starts to fall into place, the story begins.

Headlines have to grab attention but they also have to set the scene for a story. If it's a funny story, there will be a sense of that in the headline. The same with a sad story. The headline will be very short and evocative and the precede will lead the reader into the story.

The precede—or strapline or stand-first, whatever you wish to call it—is essentially a layout device to ease the reader into a story. The person who wrote the story doesn't usually write the precede that appears when the story's published. Subeditors do that. But it doesn't hurt to try to write your own precedes; it's handy for subeditors. Basically, there are two definite styles of precedes—those with the by-line, and those without. I prefer to have the by-line separate to the precede, otherwise you're limited in the scope of the precede because you have to include something like, 'as Joe Bloggs reports'.

Precedes

Precedes are short descriptions of the article, summing up what you're about to read. They have become increasingly popular over the past ten years. Usually set in a larger or bolder typeface, they often include the by-line of the article. Think of a precede as a way of introducing an article. Precedes are also known as summaries, kickers, write-offs, stand-firsts, lead-ins, leaders, straplines, title bars—it depends who you're talking to.

Like titles, precedes are usually the domain of the editor or subeditor but it certainly helps to be able to write your own precede. For a start, it makes you concisely describe what your article is about. When you are developing an idea for a story, you should be attempting to sum up the idea in just a sentence or two. This can become the basis of a precede, and also, as you will see in chapter 12, of a query letter. (If you find it difficult to sum up your story it may be because you aren't clear enough about your angle.)

The following extracts give a brief indication of how the top of a story can work.

> Title: 'Paying the bills with artistry'
> No precede.
> Lead: In 1983, Australian band Men At Work were taking the world by storm. Despite a gruelling schedule of international touring, front man, singer and songwriter Colin Hay found time to seek out a small workshop in the backstreets of East Geelong. He came to place an order with John McGrath, guitar maker. John smiles at the recollection. 'He's sort of taken that original guitar around the world many times. It's done thousands of miles with him.' (76 words.)
>
> Rob Doole, unpublished article

The lead of this profile of a local guitar-maker tells an anecdote about a famous person, sets the scene of the interview (a small workshop) and quotes the subject of the interview.

> Title: 'And it's gold, gold, gold to Australia'
> Precede: Careers in sports and recreation offer a bright future. (Nine words)
> Lead: Although still two years out from the much heralded Sydney 2000 Olympics, Australians have begun to focus on the preparations—and athletes are not the only ones under scrutiny. (30 words)
>
> (*Learn for Your Life*, a careers guide published by Victoria University of Technology, Spring 1998)

The title uses a well-known sporting phrase, while the precede simply and effectively states what the article is about. The lead uses the Sydney Olympics as an example of the importance of sports and recreation management.

There are many ways to write titles, precedes and leads. Don't be afraid to try different styles. With the top of the story under control you then have to maintain interest for the whole story, making sure your paragraphs link together, moving from one theme or incident to another, all the way to the end of the article.

Endings

A story needs to end with a sense of purpose. Endings are not afterthoughts. Endings matter. They are what readers are most likely to remember. A good lead will make a reader curious, a good ending will leave a reader satisfied.

You can end a story with many of the ingredients that you begin a story with: quotes, statements, metaphors or anecdotes, to name a few. An anecdote may begin the story, be left hanging, and then brought back to finish the story.

One of the most popular ways of ending a story is to refer to the start of the story. Finding a good lead, then, can also help

> Kate Arnold is a journalist who writes for a range of corporate clients. Her public relations work includes writing and 'doing everything' for People, Holden's national quarterly employee magazine, writing a regular newsletter for the Royal Freemason's Homes of Victoria and preparing promotional material for Gerfloor Australasia.
>
> The intro is critical to the success of the story. It sets the direction. The intro must succinctly outline the story or the wheels are likely to fall off. As a cadet journalist on a country daily I recall being under pressure to write a story for the front page of the paper. A senior colleague suggested I write the body of the story and come back to the intro. But I could never work like that. I need to feel the lead and develop my thoughts from there. The intro is what gives a story its zing and spark.
>
> I see the first paragraph as the real grit of the story, underpinned by the second. In the third para you see the story evolving.
>
> I develop a story as long as it has momentum. I don't consciously write a conclusion. Sometimes I might add something satirical or quirky or pose a question, giving the reader something to ponder.

you find a good ending. This 'circular' way of ending has also been described as tying a bow on top of a gift-wrapped package. An ending needs to wrap up the story, but it can also point to the future, or to other issues.

How-to, list and some travel stories would seem to have fairly obvious endings: when you've completed the instructions on building a letterbox, when you've reached Z in your A-to-Z article or when you've reached the end of a journey.

> Ending a story seems to be much easier than starting it. Some writers get a bit florid, a bit over the top; more of that throat-clearing syndrome. But *On the Road* is a magazine about trips, about journeys, so it's pretty obvious where many stories will finish! (Pat Hayes, editor *On the Road*)

Summary

- There are three parts to the top of a story: title, precede and lead
- The top of the story has to propel your reader into the whole story
- A good lead can help you structure the whole story
- Most readers are browsers—can you arrest their attention?
- Endings need a sense of purpose

Exercises

1. Here are five possible titles. What stories could they apply to?
    All in the family
    Brave heart
    Crowded house
    Pulp fiction
    Rebel without a cause

2. Collect ten titles from a magazine which really appeal to you. What devices have been used to get your attention?

3. Write alternative titles to the ten you collected for question 2. Aim to make yours as sharp and readable.

4. Here are two story ideas. Write two titles for each.

    A woman has left full-time teaching to start a winery.

    A home-decorating feature on innovations in bathroom design.

5. Write a title for the draft you began in chapter 9.

6. Collect five precedes that drew you into an article.

7. Identify what those precedes did to hook you.

8. Write a precede for your own draft feature article.

THE TOP AND THE TAIL OF THE STORY

9. Read three articles that do not have precedes. Write precedes for them, giving yourself a maximum of two sentences of no more than 25 words each.

10. Collect five favourite leads or use five leads from articles in appendix 1.

11. Identify how the leads kept your attention.

12. Write a lead for your own draft feature.

13. Collect five endings that were satisfying.

14. How did the endings work?

15. Write an ending for your draft feature article.

eleven Adding value to your story

In Victorian times readers may have been happy with columns and columns of text but readers now are daunted by large slabs of type.

Pat Hayes, editor, *On the Road*

Most feature articles need more than plain text. Think beyond the limits of wordage and imagine the story laid out on a magazine page. The title and precede will catch your readers' eye but there are other factors that affect how people read, and how you write, an article. You can add value to your stories by including a sidebar, a quiz, a postscript or photographs, or a combination of these.

Adding value to an article increases your chances of getting it published. It increases the attractiveness of your piece to an editor, and saves the editor work.

Sidebars

Sidebars are boxes separated from the main text of the article. They are often printed with borders around the text, or with shading. Some have a small heading or title of their own. They can also have sub-headings.

Sidebars can include facts, tips, quotes, background information: material that is important but may not fit into the main body of the article. This material can complement, expand, or zoom in and out of the story.

A feature about dementia would quote several families and specialists in the main text. There could be three sidebar possibilities: information on how to contact local, state or national support groups; a backgrounder detailing the general history of the illness; and a closer look at one of the families quoted in the main text. This last sidebar may be written from a different point of view: all in first person as a daughter recounts the story of how the illness has affected her mother and herself.

Many travel stories have sidebars with tips about general costs, safety and health. A travel story about a volatile country may include a sidebar offering advice from the Australian Department of Foreign Affairs. Profiles of celebrities may use sidebars to include extra quotes, or to give a brief chronology of the person's life. A story on an actor could have a sidebar listing the actor's main films, plus the year of each film.

Pat Hayes, editor of *On the Road*, uses sidebars throughout his magazine.

> *On the Road* is an information mag, so most of our stories have what we call Fact Files—side bars which tell you how to get there, what the facilities are, how much the camping fees are, how to contact the local ranger.
>
> We also like what we call break-out boxes—lists or anecdotes or historical and technical sidelights which don't fit into the main part of the story. Some of our articles run to eight pages, so you have to be able to break up the text.

Sidebars catch the eye. They are good for those who love to browse. Readers may read a sidebar before starting on the actual story. A reader's eye may move from the sidebar, across some text, and eventually to the whole of the story.

Sidebars also catch editors' eyes. As soon as editors know there's a sidebar they can start to visualise the page. (In studying the marketplace, you will have established that the publication regularly uses sidebars. Many articles will have sidebars, but not all.)

The length of a sidebar will depend on the length of the main article. Basically, they're short. Use your discretion. When preparing your article for an editor, type sidebars on a separate page from the main text. Simply type 'Sidebar to story on . . .' at the top of the page.

Sidebars can be the icing on the cake of your article. For readers they can be exactly what they are looking for: their appetite has been whetted by the main story but the sidebar rounds off the meal. See the 'Getting there' paragraphs in 'Georgiana's passion' in appendix 1 for an example of a sidebar.

Postscripts

A postscript, or footnote, to an article is a very small slice of extra text at the bottom of the story. Often printed in italics or bold, it will provide essential, or at least helpful, information: an address or contact number or date which does not require a sidebar. It can also include a description or the qualifications of the writer.

Quizzes

Quizzes bring readers right into the story. An article about safety in the workplace, either for a staff journal or a general publication, may be improved by having a short quiz at the end. Quizzes about personality types are very popular in women's magazines.

When planning a quiz, work backwards from the answers and devise questions around them. Don't make the answers too obvious or predictable. You want your reader to feel they've discovered something or really tested themselves. Do the quiz yourself and ask, Are the questions worded so they are easy to follow? Are the choices different enough? Be certain to include the answers!

Photographs

In studying the marketplace you would learn which publications accept photographs from contributors. Magazines at the top end of the market—the fashion, food and home glossies, for example—use their own photographers.

Smaller publications may be interested in a package deal of story plus photographs. It is not uncommon for travel writers to take their own photographs.

> *Every story in* On the Road *magazine has photographs. Editor Pat Hayes gives some tips on sending photographs with stories.*
>
> The basics of taking publishable photographs can be learnt. It's not magic, you don't have to be born with the skill. Do a local course to learn the basics.
>
> I'd suggest you think long and hard about the camera you buy. Auto-focus cameras can be quite good. You don't run the risk of out-of-focus shots, of photographs that are a little bit 'soft'.
>
> When photographing people, make sure there are no shadows on their faces—otherwise you end up with a blank, black blob which cannot be used. Have people looking into the sun; get rid of their sunglasses and take their hats off! We want to see who the people are.
>
> Check that there's nothing in the background that will detract from the photo. You don't want branches sticking out of people's heads. Make sure the foreground is also clear of distractions.
>
> Don't send too few photographs, and don't send too many. Four or five is not enough, more than twenty is too many. Make

sure there are a variety of shots: vertical, horizontal, close-ups, some with a sense of perspective.

We prefer photographs to be presented as transparencies (or slides). You get deeper colours than you do with prints. But it is more difficult to take photographs with transparencies: you have to be spot-on.

Photographs must have captions. The bane of our lives is getting photographs of, say, different mountains and not knowing which is which. Which is Mt Kosciusko and which is Mt Buffalo? Put numbers on the transparencies and type up the corresponding captions at the end of your article.

Make sure your photographs are well-protected when you send them, and include a postage-paid envelope so that the photographs are sent back to you.

We are most likely to drop a good story if there are no pics or if the pics are not good enough. With us, it's a chicken-or-the-egg argument about which comes first—the photographs or the story? The answer is both.

Series

It's possible that an idea for a story could develop into several stories. The topic of shiftwork could be too big for a single article but could become a series of profiles of the people who work while the world sleeps. See 'Georgiana's passion' and 'McGrath's guitars' in appendix 1 as examples of stories that form part of a series.

Summary

- Adding value to an article increases your chances of getting it published
- Sidebars can include facts, tips, case studies or background information

ADDING VALUE TO YOUR STORY **139**

- Sidebars are often the icing on the cake of a good article
- Postscripts are very short pieces of information at the end of an article
- Quizzes bring readers right into the story
- Check with editors before sending photographs
- Look for story ideas which could develop into several stories or a series

Exercises

1. Find three sidebars in published feature articles. Describe them.

2. Write two sidebars to go with your own article—one statistical, one a direct quote.

3. Look for three articles (not hard news stories) which do not have sidebars. Read each whole article and ask, Does the story work anyway? Outline possible sidebars for such stories.

4. Collect four quizzes. Add three questions (and answers) to those quizzes.

5. Write a ten-question quiz to accompany a story about housework. The aim of this quiz is for the reader to find out what sort of houseworker they are. Make it light.

6. Study three articles which are part of a series or a column. Why does the series have longevity? What future stories could there be in the series?

7. Revisit your ideas file—do you have ideas that could be part of a series?

8. Study the photographs in publications you aim to write for. Look at how the photo complements the story, how the elements of the photo—the people, the light, the perspective—all fit together.

twelve Presenting and selling your work

I ask people to ring with an idea, or to send an outline. This prevents disappointments if a person has written a complete story and we don't want it.

Thornton McCamish, editor, *The Big Issue*

Corresponding with editors is a vital aspect of non-fiction writing. You need to to develop a rapport with editors. They, after all, make the decisions. You must be flexible if they want to rearrange your ideas a little, and you must be thick-skinned in the face of rejection slips. You also need to understand what rights you are selling and how to negotiate payment when you sell a story to a publication.

Query letters

A query letter is an outline of your idea for a story, sent to an editor. It is a business document. Writing query letters—or proposals or outlines—is an important part of running a professional writing business.

Sending in stories 'cold' (to an editor without any previous correspondence) may be all right if the stories are short (about 1000 words or less) and do not require much research, but if you're going to work on a longer, detailed piece you'll have more confidence if you know an editor has expressed interest in your query letter.

Another advantage is that in approaching your prospective interviewees, you can quite truthfully say, '*Kite Flying Monthly* has shown interest in this piece'. This is much better than saying, 'Ah, well, um, I'm hoping to sell it to somewhere'.

A query letter is short (no longer than 350 words), formal (but not stuffy) and professionally presented (regardless of whether it's a letter, a fax or an e-mail).

A query letter needs to contain the following information:

- Your name and contact details: phone, address, e-mail and so on.
- The name and correct title of the editor. Do not send a letter that begins 'Dear Sir/Madam', or 'Dear Editor'. This immediately shows a lack of real interest in the publication. Also, a quick phonecall to the publication's front office will tell you whether editors should be addressed as Mr, Mrs, Miss or Ms.
- What the story is about. Your opening line could be like a precede, a summary of the proposed article. Alternatively, you can quickly lead the editor into the proposed story, announcing a curious fact or asking a question that you believe will get the editor's attention.
- The title of the proposed article.
- The anticipated length (approximate wordage) of the story.
- Structure of the article, including sidebars, postscripts and photographs.
- Whom you intend to interview (if not their names, then their positions).
- Your qualifications to write the piece. The quality of the

> query letter itself should prove that you can write clearly and succinctly. You may also have a specialist knowledge of the subject you're writing about.
> - When you can have the story ready or approximately how long you expect it will take to complete the article.
> - How you intend to send the final story: hard copy, on disk or e-mail. Include details of the word processing software you use.

This information does not come off the top of your head. You need to do some research before you send in a query letter, just as you need to do research for the article. You have to try to find out if the idea has weight, if it can run the distance. You can quote some of your research in the query letter, thereby showing the editor that you've done some groundwork.

Do not make the mistakes that Maree Curtis, who has worked as a section editor at *The Sunday Age* and the *Herald Sun*, has come across:

> Do not ever approach an editor if you haven't read their sections. Read a section for weeks and weeks to get a feel for the type of stuff that's been run and what's been run already.
>
> People have rung me up and said, 'I've got a story I know you'll love', but I'd run a similar story the week before. When you approach an editor, remember the envelope you address and the letter you send tells the editor something about you. Make sure you're accurate.
>
> I once had a letter addressed to Marie Curtin, Body and Soul—instead of Maree Curtis, Mind & Body. I didn't read the rest—how can I believe anything in this person's story will be right if they haven't made sure my name, my section and the publication is right? It's sloppy and it's also insulting.

A successful query letter

Here is an example of a query letter which at first received no response from a section editor at *The Australian*. The query letter was just slightly revised and faxed to the Observer editor at the same paper. (Observer is a column that often runs essay-like articles by contributors.) The second editor rang within an hour and accepted the idea.

Jim Buckell　　　　　　　　　　Name
Observer Editor　　　　　　　　Address
The Australian　　　　　　　　Telephone/Fax
15 December 1997

The Summer Songs of Paul Kelly

Dear Mr Buckell,

What are some of the great images of the Australian summer? Russell Drysdale's painting *The Cricketers*. Max Dupain's photographs at Newport Beach. Ray Lawler's play *The Summer of the Seventeenth Doll*. Helen Garner's city heat in *Monkey Grip*. Robert Drewe's stories in *The Bodysurfers*.

It is time songwriter Paul Kelly was recognised for his depictions of summer. Kelly has said that he mainly writes about love, sex and death. When you include summer within those topics you find a series of songs that are as definitive as the works of Drysdale, Dupain, Garner, Lawler, Drewe and others.

When Kelly sings about summer he also sings about cricket, bushfires, ice-cream, Christmas, gaol, parenthood and childhood sweethearts.

Just look at the cover of his greatest hits album, *Songs from the South*: a beach, a boy, a cricket bat. A quintessential Australian image.

I propose an 800 to 1000 word article describing and quoting

> the summer songs of Paul Kelly. The structure of the article could be that of a 100–200 word intro, followed by a discussion of ten of Kelly's songs. The songs to be discussed are:
> - 'Standing on the Street of Early Sorrow' (from the 1985 *Post* album)
> - 'Bradman' (1987, *Under the Sun*)
> - 'I Can't Believe We Were Married' (1991, *Comedy*)
> - 'Summer Rain' (1994, *Wanted Man*)
> - 'Song from the Sixteenth Floor' (1994, *Wanted Man*)
> - 'Deeper Water' (1995, *Deeper Water*)
> - 'Blush' (1995, *Deeper Water*)
> - 'How to Make Gravy' (1996)
> - 'Melting' (1997)
> - 'Behind the Bowler's Arm' (?)
>
> I could complete the story within a week of hearing from you. The story will be sent on hard copy, via fax.
>
> Yours sincerely . . . .

Why was this query letter successful? First of all, it is short: 286 words. Now look at the date and the working title. The idea is seasonal, the letter was submitted early in summer. The working title sums up the theme, though the title is not strong enough to be a published headline. The publication is national, as is the theme of the article: an Australian songwriter singing about Australian summers.

The opening sentence of the letter poses a question to the editor and then answers it. The second paragraph states the theme of the article. The third paragraph backs up this theme with some evidence. The fourth paragraph concludes the theme and also, indirectly, provides a suggestion for a possible photograph to accompany the piece.

The fifth paragraph gets to the nuts and bolts: word length and structure. The writer has examined other Observer articles and knows the limits of the word length. The suggested structure shows the writer has a concrete idea of how to present the material (even, though, the structure did change a little in the published article).

Finally, the list of songs proves to the editor that the writer has done some research and already knows the topic well. One song was omitted from the final draft because it didn't quite fit the theme of summer songs.

While this is a short article, the writer still needed time to chase up some facts, especially dates concerning the artists and writers referred to in the opening paragraph of the proposal (which became the basis of the opening paragraphs of the final article). The writer wanted to write the story with the confidence of an editor's approval. And confidence is a key factor in writing—it gives you momentum.

The editor's response to this query letter was immediate. He had published the writer previously, so had faith in the writer's ability to deliver. The agreed wordage was a maximum of 900 words. The deadline was flexible and, in the end, the writer did not submit the story until 30 December. It appeared, with the heading, 'Under the sun in Kelly country', on 5 January 1998. A photograph of the CD cover of *Songs from the South* accompanied the story. This article is in appendix 1.

Following up the query letter

Having sent a query letter, you hope for a quick, affirmative reply. Generally, a magazine editor is likely to take longer to respond to you than the editor of a newspaper supplement. (There is no fixed time, no standard arrangement in these matters.) You may not get a reply at all, depending on the busy-ness of the editor, the strength—or weakness—of the idea, and the timing of the query letter.

It is often helpful to contact an editor a week after you've sent a letter just to check that it has arrived. There's the possibility that the editor hunts out your letter there and then and gives you an immediate response. Or, the editor may ask you to describe the idea straight away. You must be prepared! Have your copy of the query letter in front of you when you make the phone call.

It's quite likely you will be talking to voicemail, so make sure you are organised and know what to say.

If you cannot get a reply in good time—and this is important for topical pieces—then you are quite entitled to send your query letter elsewhere.

But let's be positive. Say the editor does get back to you quickly and does want the story. You've got the go-ahead to write the story but the editor is unlikely to promise to publish the story. You've shown you can write a query letter, now you have to prove you can come up with the final product.

The editor may make suggestions for angling the story more towards the publication. The word length may be an issue (although, because you know your market, you will have an understanding of what's required), or the editor may want different information in the sidebar. Also clarify and agree to a rate of pay before proceeding with the article.

It is vital that you and the editor have a very clear idea of what is to be written. Otherwise, you may go to a lot of trouble and end up with an article that is not quite what the editor expected—or not at all what the editor expected.

Changing focus midstream

Sometimes the focus of an idea may change while you are working on the story. In this case it is best to contact the editor and discuss the direction of the story. Once, while working on a story about drive-ins, which an editor had agreed to after reading the query letter, the writer discovered that a sidebar could really lift the story. The writer knew that the sidebar—briefly detailing the history of about 25 old drive-ins—would require a number of phone calls. The writer contacted the editor in the middle of writing the main story, got the go-ahead for the sidebar, and then made close to 50 phone calls!

Thornton McCamish is editor of The Big Issue. *Here he recounts some experiences working with prospective contributors.*

I ask people to ring with an idea, or to send an outline—one paragraph on your 'angle' is plenty. This prevents disappointments if a person has written a complete story and we don't want it. If we like the idea, we will call you to discuss it further. This process helps you to prevent wasting your time writing articles which—however masterful their prose style—are innappropriate for our mag.

We would encourage you not to be disheartened if your first ideas are not picked up. Basically, we don't put someone on a story unless we are confident that it would suit the magazine . . .

I'm startled by the incompetency of some approaches. People will ring up with an idea for a lifestyle story that's totally inappropriate for *The Big Issue*. They will have no idea what the magazine is, and haven't even bothered to know who to talk to. Or people send in letters with spelling mistakes.

One person wrote, 'I hope to one day write for *Time* and *Newsweek* but I'm happy to write for *The Big Issue* for the time being . . .' Another person wrote, 'I'm not a clever clogs but I'd like to write an editorial'. Sometimes I hear from very bossy freelancers who demand I run their story and pay them immediately. They get all snooty at the most polite rejection letter.

We receive more ideas than ready-made stories, and I always commission several pieces. I try not to send bland rejection letters

> but sometimes you just have to, if the story or idea is so poorly presented.
>
> Having said all that, the most satisfying part of being an editor is collaborating with the writers, working an idea into a published feature.

Presenting query letters and articles

Query letters and articles are pieces of professional correspondence. Keep everything clean and clear. Don't try to impress the editor with superficialities such as fancy fonts, coloured print and elaborate letterheads. If you are sending material in on hard copy (the industry jargon for paper) remember the basic rules:

- Double-space the text (which means a double space between the lines of the text, not between every word).
- Give your page wide margins.
- Number your pages.
- Put your name and contact details on the first and last pages.
- Put the name of the editor on the top of every page, plus a key word from your title. (Word-processing programs have what are known as headers and footers. These can help you in placing this 'identifying' material on the page. Make sure you are consistent with presentation.)
- Paper-clip the pages, do not use staples.
- If you're posting the material, be sure to use a good-sized envelope. An editor doesn't want to open a letter that has been stuffed into a too-small envelope.
- Include a stamped self-addressed envelope for the editor's reply.

Before sending material via e-mail, check the publications policy on 'attachments'—a word processed document that is sent along with your e-mail message. Some computers can automatically delete attachments because they can carry viruses. Remember to keep accurate records of all your correspondence.

Rejections

Sooner or later you will receive rejection slips for your query letters or stories sent in cold. There are several reasons why material is rejected:

- The idea is boring.
- The story is too long.
- It's too short.
- It's too late.
- It's littered with spelling mistakes.
- It's been sent to the wrong editor.
- The editor has no space in upcoming issues.
- The editor has no money for more contributors.
- The story is nearly good enough, but not quite.

Now, very few editors have the time to tell you why your material is rejected. The most common form of correspondence from an editor in these matters is the rejection slip—a short note that simply says something like, 'Please find enclosed your material, which we are unable to use on this occasion'. Or: 'After considering the article carefully I've decided to decline, with thanks. Maybe you can place it elsewhere.'

Occasionally, an editor will make the time to reply to you in a more detailed manner: 'Your story would have been perfect for a mental health special we're running in the current issue, but we didn't get it in time to consider it.' Or: 'While I feel your idea has some merit, I cannot see an easy opportunity for our using it. We have a very tight schedule and limited editorial space. Accordingly, I am returning it, with regret.'

Do not take rejection slips personally. Look at them professionally. If you can't find a home for your idea after three attempts, review the query letter, or the story. Try to be objective. Put yourself in the editor's shoes and ask, 'Why doesn't this appeal?'

Regular work

Once you're making regular contact with editors who are publishing your stories, you can ring them with ideas. Write down your ideas before you ring. Formalise them, don't just rattle things off the top of your head. Be organised. Once confidence and rapport have been established, you can also send several ideas to an editor, summing up the ideas very briefly.

Selling a story more than once

When you send a story to a publication (either 'cold' or after a successful query letter), you are effectively offering that publication certain rights to publish the story. Some editors may discuss these matters formally, others presume that if you've sent a story, for example, to a publication with a statewide readership, then you have offered state rights. For a national publication, you are offering national rights. If you send the story to an overseas publication you are offering the national rights to publish in that particular country. To make these matters official you simply need to include a covering letter stating what rights you are offering to the publication.

You are also entitled to sell the story to other publications as long as the readerships do not overlap, and the publications are not in direct competition with each other. For example, you could write a gardening story for a South

Australian publication, then rewrite it slightly for Western Australian and Victorian publications. You must tell editors if the story has been published elsewhere.

Some freelance writers regularly publish their stories several times, inside and outside of Australia. It usually requires some rewriting of the original story. Multiselling stories can be very profitable.

Negotiating payment

As we mentioned in chapter 2, payment will vary between publications and, sometimes, between editors within publication. Before selling your story, ask what the publication pays. You will usually be quoted a rate per word. Work out beforehand what an acceptable minimum rate is for you. Don't let the excitement of getting published cloud your judgement.

Refer to the Australian Journalists' Association's rates for freelancers. Compare notes with other non-fiction writers about rates of pay. This should give you an idea of what to expect.

Summary

- A query letter is an outline of your idea for a story
- It is a piece of professional correspondence
- Be accurate with names of editors and publications, and with everything else
- It is vital that you and the editor have a very clear idea of how the idea is to be developed into a story
- Inform the editor if the focus is changing midstream
- Keep records of all correspondence with editors
- Bear in mind that there are many reasons for rejection slips
- Consider selling your story more than once
- Negotiate a realistic and fair rate of payment

Exercises

1. Write a query letter for a published story from your regular reading. Address it to the editor of the magazine or supplement where you saw the story. Sum up the article in terms of the elements of a query letter. Keep the length down to 350 words or less.

2. Write a query letter based on a story from appendix 1.

3. Write a query letter for an article you have already written.

4. Write a query letter for an idea you've been working on.

5. Do a role-play with classmates, presenting a query letter verbally to an editor. Be prepared for the editor's possible responses.

6. Swap roles—now you're the editor.

thirteen You are a published writer

What became clear during research for my book on Australian markets for writers was that there is a real need for articles written by skilled freelancers who are aware of the basic journalism and feature-writing techniques. Editors continually stressed to me that writers need to study the publication, be aware of its demographic breakdown, then write in a style which will appeal to its readership.

Rhonda Whitton, freelance journalist and editor of *The Australian Writer's Marketplace: the Complete Guide to Being Published*

Perseverance is very important. I've run pieces by young writers who have been trying for a year. I know that sooner or later they'll crack it.

Jim Buckell, former Time & Tide editor, *The Australian*

Your query letter is accepted. You write the article, send it in, and then wait. A few days, weeks, or months later the story is published. Your by-line stares back at you. You are a published writer.

After the initial excitement, you sit down and read the story slowly. The title and the precede have been changed, but you anticipated that. There are some other changes: 'color' is now 'colour'; that fancy bit of word-play has been cut; a quote has been paraphrased; the paragraphs are shorter—many of them single sentences. The story is still yours, it still looks good and the editor is pleased with it, but you have this nagging question: why the changes?

The importance of subediting

Welcome to the world of subediting. It is inevitable that your story will change in the journey from the finished story on your desk to the published article in a newspaper, magazine or journal. It is important to understand why these changes are made and to take heed of them.

Subeditors have several tasks. They:

- design and lay out pages, ensuring the article will fit an allotted space
- write headlines or titles
- write precedes
- check the grammatical and structural aspects of the story and rewrite some parts if necessary
- check facts that seem inconsistent
- check for legal problems (essentially, whether the story contains potentially defamatory material)

Major newspapers and magazines have subeditors who work on these tasks full-time. Smaller publications, including some corporate or local government publications, may have an editor who attends to these duties as well as general editing.

Not all editors or subeditors will contact you to talk about changes that need to be made. They have enough on their plate and your story is just one of many they are finetuning.

If the story is a little shorter, it may be because some advertising has been sold for the same page as your story. Do not protest, for it is the advertising that is paying for your cheque. Another reason for changes could be the design of the page. The subeditor may have taken one of the quotes in the story and highlighted it in larger text. (This is known as a 'break-out quote' or a 'pull-out quote'.) Or the photographs may take precedence over some paragraphs.

Changes in spelling will be due to the style of the publication. You may have spelt out a number—'one hundred' and it is now '100'.

Appreciate why changes are made and you will know exactly what to do when you write the next article for that publication.

The next story, and the next, and the next . . .

With one story under your belt you will have the confidence to write another. The confidence in getting published will help not just the actual writing but all that precedes it—the idea, the query letter, the research, the interviewing, the contact with editors. Getting published also helps in dealing with rejection letters—you know that they are not the end of the world.

Be careful to make sure your standards do not drop. You do not want to become a one-hit wonder. Jim Buckell, former editor of Time & Tide at *The Australian*, has seen this several times.

> Some new writers send in a cracker of a piece, which I run. Then they send in very ordinary stuff. That first story may have had lots of eyes over it—criticism from lecturers and fellow students—whereas the subsequent pieces don't appear to have the same sort of attention. Or maybe the writer only had one good idea.
>
> I also get the feeling that some stories have been vetted by family and friends and that's not a good idea. You need someone who can criticise your work.

After being published several times in the one publication you should try to branch out and send ideas to other publications. You're hoping to develop a working relationship with several editors. Eventually, they may approach you with ideas for stories for their publication. This is called 'commissioning' an article. But it is not an editor's responsibility to look after you. Their main interest is their publication.

Editors do not always stay with the same publication. If they move, you may be able to write for their next publication. There are no guarantees. A new editor may take over a section you've been writing for. That new editor is not bound to publish your stories. You have to be prepared for such changes. By being regularly published in several publications you lessen the risk of being stranded when editors do move.

Write well, write professionally, and you will be published again and again. And again.

Summary

- Your published story will be subedited
- Take heed of the subeditor's changes
- Being published increases confidence
- Do not be a one-hit wonder
- Work with several editors

Exercises

1. Study the two stories in appendix 1 about women jockeys. The first is the original story, the second is the published version. Note the changes made by the subeditor.

2. Using what we've covered in previous chapters, draw up some workshopping guidelines for how you would judge a feature article.

3. Apply your guidelines to the two articles on the guitar maker in appendix 1. Identify the differences between the two, their relative strengths and weaknesses.

appendix one Selected articles

'McGrath's guitars' by Paul Daffey

Rhythms, September 1997

This is the second part of the series on instrument-makers.

John McGrath, a 38-year-old guitar-maker from Geelong, says most of his clients have played the best mass-produced guitars and they want something more individual. Many of his orders, therefore, include decorative work.

'They're probably built for guys who've had their Martins and their Gibsons and are not quite satisfied', he says. 'They want a little extra I suppose.'

The little extra for Rod Freeman-Smith of former Melbourne band The Club Foot was a goat's head inlay for the Capricorn star sign on the headstock of the guitar in abalone and pearl. 'With the companion planet which happened to be Saturn,' McGrath says.

The goat's head added 15 hours on to the 100 hours he usually takes to make a guitar. The price starts at $3500 and rises depending on ornamentation, pick-ups for amplifiers and choice of wood.

McGrath was well-acquainted with wood by the time he started playing the guitar at 11-years-old. His father was a carpenter. 'I guess the connection was made at some point between the two. For a long time all I wanted to do was build guitars.'

He started building his first guitar as a 20-year-old while living at Port Campbell on Victoria's south-west coast. It remained unfinished until a friend told him there was an instrument-maker at Warrnambool, just up the road. Under the guidance of Steve Gilchrist, a world-renowned mandolin-maker who was featured in last month's *Rhythms*, McGrath finished his guitar and spent a year learning his craft.

Part of his education was poring over books and catalogues. In the beginning it was *The Steel String Guitar* by Donald Brosnac and *The Steel String Guitar: Construction and Repair* by David Russell Young. He studied the work of John D'Angelico, a jazz guitar-maker from New York and D'Angelico's protégé James D'Aquisto, all the while building his library of books and catalogues.

Back in Port Campbell, one of McGrath's neighbors was Russell Deppler, the manager of Men At Work. Deppler brought singer and guitarist Colin Hay around for a look at McGrath's work and Hay bought a guitar on the spot. It has remained his guitar of choice all through his solo years. In fact, Hay regards the guitar as special enough to warrant an extra ticket when he flies so that the guitar can sit up next to him.

Hay now lives in Los Angeles. His North American friends include Jeff Smallwood, a singer and guitarist from Montreal who liked Hay's guitar so much he wanted to buy it. Hay rejected the offer and advised him to ring McGrath in Geelong and order one, which he did.

In Victoria, McGrath makes guitars for Shane O'Mara of Rebecca's Empire, Alex Burns of the pub blues duo Burns And Charles, and Terry Dean and Gary Carruthers, the covers duo who have been a staple in Melbourne pubs for well over a decade. Recently he received a postcard from Taiwan where

Paul Wookey plays bluegrass in a theme park using a McGrath guitar. McGrath says bluegrass is his favourite, if he has to choose, but he likes pretty much all kinds of music.

Like most instruments made in Australia, the materials for his guitars have done a fair trip before they start travelling back to the customer as the finished product. McGrath gets his pearl from Darwin, red abalone from California and abalone in vivid blues, greens and purples from New Zealand. Blackwood is salvaged from the debris after tree-felling in the Otways and the spruce is gathered by an eccentric supplier who lives on an island off the coast of Alaska.

McGrath says spruce logs measuring two metres in diameter and up to 35 metres long were used to block rivers in Alaska to form salmon traps. Since this practice has been banned, many logs have drifted down the rivers and into the ocean. McGrath's supplier trawls the coast looking for the logs that have been washed up. McGrath has never met the supplier but photos reveal a wild-haired Grizzly Adams character.

'It's a summer hobby for him,' McGrath says. 'He's actually a carpenter. He calls me up at ungodly hours. He hasn't got the time difference down.'

This lack of attention to detail must strike instrument-makers as peculiar. It is their lot to be fastidious, which is one reason why they are so highly valued by discerning musicians.

'Paying the bills with artistry' by Rob Doole

Unpublished

In 1983, Australian band Men At Work were taking the world by storm. Despite a gruelling schedule of international touring, front man, singer and songwriter Colin Hay found time to seek out a small workshop in the back streets of East Geelong. He came to place an order with John McGrath the guitar-maker. John smiles at the recollection. 'He's sort of taken that original guitar around the world many times, it's done thousands of miles with him.'

Guitar-making is like an addiction for John. After making the first one he just felt a compulsion to keep doing it. It is obviously something that he has difficulty explaining to anyone else. 'I made a couple of guitars and then I worked for Steven Gilchrist for twelve months . . . I made the decision that I was going to go home, set up a small workshop and teach myself how to build and repair guitars. I've been doing it full-time ever since. That was fifteen years ago.'

That sale generated interest in John's guitars as far afield as Canada but even with that kind of prestige it's not easy to make the art and craft of guitar-making function as a business. 'You get ten orders and you're working by yourself, there's your year cut out for you,' he says. 'You haven't got time to scratch yourself, let alone anything else when you're doing it as a solo operation.'

Sitting in John's kitchen with a cup of coffee, the nature of the true craftsman is evident. Renovations are nearly complete—polished timber floors, everything tasteful, neat and precise. One-year-old James has just gone to bed and John's partner Glenda, a well-known local singer and songwriter, joins us.

He speaks quietly of his work and the business and lifestyle that go with it. Yet there is no false modesty. He knows the worth of his skills and the irony of having to market them in a world of mass production.

According to John, the freedom of working alone is a two-edged sword. 'It's good in a way. A lot of people have the idea that, you know, you work from home, sort of cruise around, hang out, drink cups of tea all day or whatever. But it doesn't really work like that, not once things start happening and all of a sudden you've got mortgages and children. And the only income that you're generating is from what you do for eight hours a day or whatever. All of a sudden your priorities change radically. At the end of the week you have to have basically what's needed.'

The workshop at the back of the house is neat, clean and purpose built. Shelves of exotic woods and guitar parts line the walls. A humidifier runs 24 hours a day to control the rate of moisture loss from the timber. There are some common woodworking tools as well as many highly specialised ones. Partially built instruments in various jigs and fixtures display the intricacies of the guitar-maker's craft.

As a child, John learnt the fundamentals of woodworking from his father, a carpenter. The rest he has had to find out for himself along the way. 'There's aspects of a whole lot of different things combined . . . the very fine tolerances in regard to woodworking are along the lines of pattern-making, working in thousandths of an inch. But then there's also the freedom of boat-building—like bending sides and fitting pieces, things like that. Then there's the whole sort of decorative aspect as well, like pearl inlay. And then finishing, that's a whole technology in itself.'

His customers range from serious amateur players to full-time working musicians, and the guitars take from 60 to 150 hours to complete, depending on the amount of embellishment involved. Despite his dedication to his work and the respect of his clients—who, after all part with substantial amounts of money to own one of his creations—he is realistic about how a business such as his is perceived outside the music industry. 'I don't know how you'd go getting a business loan to start up a guitar facility of any description. It's kind of like somebody asking you, "Well, what do you do for a living?" and you say, "I make guitars" and they say, "Well, what do you really do?"'

'This industry, if you want to call it an industry, hasn't really been taken all that seriously by the public at large. It doesn't have the sort of tradition in Australia. Whereas in Europe and maybe the States it does. Violin-making, in Europe especially, goes back three or four hundred years. But you could say that about the whole music scene in Australia anyway.'

But of course, anybody with the patience to create guitars like John's is prepared to take the long view in business. 'It's starting to happen. You're starting to get people out there who recognise what people are doing and take it a lot more seriously.

'You've only got to look at someone like Maton. They're making over three and a half thousand guitars a year. And you go up there and visit them and they're not playing games—it's a pretty serious kind of operation.'

John has been building guitars full-time for most of his adult life. In an economic climate where more than half of all small businesses are expected to fail in their first two years, he is philosophical about what it takes to survive in such a labour-intensive craft. 'You want to make it a lifestyle . . . it's all kind of relative, as to what you're accustomed to, how much money you need for each week. You just sort of maintain low overheads and do the work.'

What is important to John is how his guitars perform in the hands of their owners. So what does Colin Hay think of his? John smiles. 'About a year ago, he decided that he wanted to get another one. I'm in the process of building that one at the moment.'

'How to stop putting it off' by Gina Perry

Women's Health, November 1998

You know the feeling—a combination of dread and fear. Dread because that deadline is looming, and fear because you haven't even made a start. Gina Perry shows you how to get on with things.

1. Make a list
Write down all the things you are putting off. Whether it's compiling a report for your boss, giving quotes to clients, writing your last essay for a course, putting together a job application, knitting a jumper or writing a long-overdue letter—put it down on the list.

Decide how big each task is. Sometimes, putting off an unpleasant or unrewarding task makes good sense. After all, there's a chance that if you put it off long enough—someone else might step in and do it for you!

2. Focus on the 'musts'
Concentrate on the task, or tasks, that will make your life a lot easier once they're done, and those that can incur costs or penalties if they're not completed.

If not doing your tax return is going to result in a hefty fine, or not putting in a résumé might cost you a good job, then put such tasks at the top of your list.

3. Don't punish yourself
Make a list of all the things that you haven't put off doing and stick it up on the bathroom mirror. When you get depressed, or feel that you are the world's worst procrastinator, cheer yourself up by reading the list.

4. Face your fears
Consider closely the task that needs to be done most urgently and ask yourself: Why am I avoiding it? Take the time to

assess what it is about this particular task that worries you. What skills and resources do you need to get it done?

5. One step at a time
Don't allow yourself to feel overwhelmed by the extent of the task—break it down into a series of small steps. Keep each step simple and achievable. Take one step at a time and reward yourself as you complete each step.

6. Get help
If you're procrastinating because the task appears too difficult, then enlist the help of a friend or pay someone else to do it.

7. No one's perfect
If you fear that you won't do the task well enough, tell yourself it doesn't need to be done perfectly. The main thing is that you get it done.

Surely, not doing something at all is worse than not doing it as well as you would have liked.

8. Understand yourself
Be prepared to discover things about yourself. Understanding why you put off doing things is crucial. Once you've identified what it is that causes you to procrastinate, you can do something about it.

9. It's easy
The longer you put off doing something, the bigger the task becomes in your mind. But you may find that once you start it, it turns out to be easier than you thought.

10. Celebrate success
Celebrate when you start the task you have put off for so long. And always celebrate when you finish it.

'Putting it off' by Gina Perry

The Herald, 19 September 1990

Dealing with the fine art of procrastinating can no longer be put off, according to Gina Perry who looks at tactics to help people delay no more.

Allan left school at the age of 15 to become an apprentice carpenter. At 25, he left the firm he'd been with since he began his apprenticeship to start up his own business.

His boss was sorry to see Allan go and promised him a job if he ever decided to come back.

Allan had established a good reputation for himself among his clients and workmates as a hardworking, skilled tradesman. Once out on his own, requests for quotes were steady. Going round to clients' properties and measuring up was no problem, but when it came to following through with a written quote he just kept putting it off.

'At the end of the first month I'd been out to look at six jobs, and I didn't have a go ahead to start on any of them,' he said. 'I had some letterheads printed, I tidied up my workshop, I even had a sign painted to put on the front fence, but all the time, in the back of my mind, I knew I had to send off those quotes or I'd be out of business before I even started.

'Finally the bank rang to say they wouldn't extend my overdraft. In the end, I got on the phone and I had to lie. I rang a few clients and said that the quote had been lost in the mail. A number of them, of course, had already found someone else to do the job for them.'

Marie, 36, is an academic in a temporary position at a university. When a permanent position became vacant in her department it was clearly earmarked for her. She had four weeks before the applications closed and she kept putting off preparing her application.

She knew she should have been working on it, but suddenly there seemed a whole range of other trivial things that she felt she should do first. At the end of the closing day for applications, her boss rang her, horrified that her letter would not arrive in time.

Kerrin Howard and Leonie Elphinstone, two Melbourne psychologists, have run groups for the past three years for people like Marie and Allan who have a problem with procrastination.

People often blame their procrastination on laziness, an inability to get organised, even both, but Kerrin says there is often far more to it than that.

She sees procrastinators as generally motivated by fear. It can be very helpful, she says, to encourage people to finish a sentence beginning with 'If I complete this thing I have been putting off for so long, I'm frightened that . . .'

Leonie, who is also a Learning Skills counsellor at RMIT [Royal Melbourne Institute of Technology], often sees successful students who, nearing the end of their course, just can't seem to meet their course deadlines any more. They are fearful, she says, of the end of their course because of the changes it will bring.

'Part-time students in particular spend a long time doing their degrees. Finishing that degree, which they've fitted into their lives often with full-time work, family commitments and so on, can mean a drastic change in their lives, their relationships and their roles. Successful completion of their course means that they will also have to make decisions about the next part of their lives.'

Procrastination is used by these people to sabotage their success.

Allan places himself in this category. 'When I really think about it, I guess I had mixed feelings about working on my own, about developing business skills, about assuming a new role in my work.

'I knew the safety net of my old job was always there if I needed it. All of a sudden I had this feeling, like, OK now you're an adult. You're on your own. And that was scary.'

Some people procrastinate because they are afraid of failure, Kerrin says, rather than success. They are afraid of not doing well enough.

Marie believes that the fact that she was offered her first tutoring job in the department when she was still a postgraduate student established high expectations among the other staff about her abilities. When the position came up that would have been a promotion for her, she felt it would test her ability.

'By putting it off to the last minute like that, I could continue to kid myself that if I really wanted to, I could have done a brilliant application. If I'd put a lot of effort into it and failed, it would have been dreadful,' she said.

'If I didn't put too much effort into it at all, then I had an excuse. I could have got the job if I'd worked harder.'

Kerrin says that Marie, like many procrastinators, is frightened of measuring up to her own high standards. By procrastinating, she has avoided a real test of her ability. In putting off making a start, she could put off any view of failing. Not having done it was quite different from having done it, and not having done it well.

Some procrastination doesn't fit so easily into one category. In Pam's case, it was due to a combination of reasons.

At 30, she had recently completed an adult education class in poetry. Her teacher encouraged her to send a poem to a prestigious literary magazine and Pam was amazed when the editor wrote back suggesting a couple of changes, but encouraging her to re-submit it, saying he was 'very interested' in her work.

For Pam, rather than being an inspiration and an encouragement, 'It caused instant writer's block. That poem's been lying on my desk now for eight months. I haven't touched it.'

For Pam it was fear of success that kept her from rewriting and finishing the poem. Success was daunting. One poem set a precedent.

'If I succeeded, if I wrote a fabulous poem, and they accepted it, then I'd have to keep writing fabulous poems,' she said.

On the other hand, she was frightened of not doing well enough, was plagued by self doubt and worried that '. . . perhaps, deep down, your potential isn't as great as everyone told you it would be. Everyone else has these expectations of you which you really can't fulfill.'

Still others, Kerrin says, procrastinate as a way of 'thumbing their noses' at authority. Procrastination at work is a powerful way of telling your boss/colleague: 'I'll do it in my own time, not in a time you specify.' It gives the procrastinator a sense of power in a situation where he/she may feel powerless.

So what's the answer? Leonie says the first crucial step is make sure you are procrastinating, and not just delaying an unpleasant task.

'Postponing can be very rational. If you delay doing something because you know that someone else is likely to step in and do it for you, that can be quite sensible,' she said.

'On the other hand, procrastination is when you put off doing something that you know you can't get out of. You recognise the necessity of doing it yet you go ahead and do something else.

'It's procrastination when the price of delaying doing the task is high. You may end up with a beautifully clean house, but the price is a failed exam.'

Whether it's a way of gaining power, avoiding failure, or sabotaging success, procrastination buffers shaky self esteem, she says. Recognising what your procrastination is protecting you from is enough to get most people going again, Leonie says.

'Procrastinators feel confused and bewildered by their own

behaviour. Once people understand why they're procrastinating they feel an enormous sense of relief. This frees them up to act, to get on with the task they've agonised over not doing for so long.'

For Allan, a short course in business management and some practical coaching in negotiating skills strengthened his confidence and reduced his need to procrastinate.

Marie found that keeping a diary of when she procrastinated was useful in helping to see the link between her procrastination and irrational thinking that fed it.

'I realised that I had a constant feeling of never being able to measure up—and no wonder. Not only did I expect myself to be perfect at all times, but I also assumed that my work colleagues expected the same impossibly high standards,' she said. 'Once you see that down on paper, you realise how ridiculous it is.'

Breaking the tasks she was putting off into smaller, more achievable steps was the key for Pam.

'I'd been associating finishing that one poem with having to write a whole string of them—all of them equally wonderful, of course. When I was able to look at it as taking one step at a time, as finishing the one and sending it off as an achievement in itself, I actually enjoyed sitting down at my desk and doing it.'

'Georgiana's passion' by Mary Ryllis Clark

Age, 18 May 1996

Georgiana McCrae's heart broke when she had to leave her beloved 'Mountain Home'. Today it is a national treasure, writes Mary Ryllis Clark.

In October 1851, at the age of 47, the artist Georgiana McCrae wrote in her now famous journal of the deep sorrow in her heart: '. . . for a few days hence I must bid farewell to my Mountain Home—and forsake the garden I had formed and the trees that I planted.'

Georgiana's distress went beyond having to leave the home she had designed herself on the shores of Port Phillip Bay at the base of Arthur's Seat. It was almost certainly the final realisation that life with her restless husband, Andrew McCrae, would always follow the same pattern: enthusiasm for a new venture, heavy financial outlay (but never enough), a period of adjusting and settling down, followed by debt, disillusionment and departure.

In 1838, the McCraes met Major Thomas Mitchell in London and Andrew discovered a new enthusiasm—Australia. His career as a lawyer was going nowhere and he was in financial difficulties. The couple had moved several times since their marriage in 1830 and, in 1838, Andrew embarked for the colonies, followed in 1840 by Georgiana.

Within 13 years, the McCraes twice created new lives for themselves and their children in the Port Phillip district of their new country, and twice Georgiana was forced to leave a house and an existence she loved.

Andrew first attempted to make his fortune by establishing a legal practice in early Melbourne. At first, all went well and Georgiana designed an elegant home, Mayfield, on the banks of the Yarra at Abbotsford.

Soon after writing an article on the McCraes in June

1993, I received a phone call from a man who had visited Mayfield in the early 1950s and, although it was run down, he was struck by the beauty of the house. He especially remembered the hand-painted flower patterns on the doors.

Tragically, Mayfield was demolished soon after to make way for a chocolate factory. Fortunately, the same fate did not befall the family's second home in Port Phillip. The Arthur's Seat home was also designed by Georgiana and again, to her surprise, she was very happy there. She adapted well to the isolation of the bush, but still retained the values of her background—a good education for her children, daily prayers for the household, lively hospitality and music.

In her biography *Georgiana*, recently re-released by Melbourne University Press in paperback, Brenda Niall describes Georgiana as being totally lacking in class consciousness and enjoying the company of the local Bunurong people, itinerant travellers and farming neighbours, as well as visits from her friends in Melbourne, including Superintendent Charles La Trobe.

The McCrae years at Arthur's Seat were, says Brenda, 'probably the happiest period the family ever experienced. The children learned classics from their tutor and all manner of bush skills from the Bunurong people, with whom they co-existed very happily.'

But Andrew lacked the capital to clear and stock the land, much of which was rocky and unusable. Again he fell into debt. He sold the lease and improvements to Joseph Burrell for 1000 pounds and accepted a position as police magistrate in remote Alberton, in Gippsland.

Georgiana returned to Melbourne with the children. The family never lived together again.

Andrew held a series of government positions in rural Victoria while Georgiana stayed in Melbourne, becoming a formidable presence in literary and artistic circles. Her hopes for a legacy from her family were dashed and, to her own financial detriment and the horror of Melbourne society, she insisted on a legal separation from her husband in 1867. She had, according to Brenda Niall, had enough of Andrew McCrae.

Although Georgiana lived until 1890 in Collingwood, Richmond and East Melbourne, the McCrae name is forever associated with the Mountain Home at Arthur's Seat that Georgiana loved so much. The Burrell family lived there for 74 years, eventually subdividing most of the original landholding in 1919 and the rest in 1925, on the death of Joseph's daughter, Kathrine.

Astonishingly, the timber homestead survived the development of the township of McCrae. There were a series of owners after the Burrells until 1961, when it was bought back into the McCrae family by Andrew and Georgiana's great-grandson, George Gordon McCrae. Brenda Niall believes this romantic gesture was a direct result of growing up with stories passed down in the family about the idyllic time at Arthur's Seat.

It was because of George Gordon that the house is now a national treasure. He gathered together many of the original McCrae furnishings and family possessions, and opened the house as a museum. After George Gordon's death in 1970, the house, now known as the McCrae Homestead, was sold on generous terms to the National Trust by his son, Andrew McCrae.

In the early 1970s, the National Trust restored the homestead, guided by Georgiana's numerous sketches of the building and garden, and her detailed floor plan of the house that noted all the furnishings and the use of every room.

In January this year, the National Trust opened a museum next to the homestead. The centre contains many of Georgiana's exquisite watercolours, drawings of the homestead, some of the furniture she brought from England and a striking portrait of her in old age. Right until the end, Georgiana would refer to her love of Arthur's Seat and the ache in her heart at the loss of her garden.

GETTING THERE

The McCrae Homestead is in Charles Street, McCrae on the Mornington Peninsula, about 75 kilometres from Melbourne along the Nepean Highway. It is well sign-posted.

The homestead and museum centre are open every day, except Christmas Day, from noon to 4.30 pm. Groups by appointment at other times. For further information, contact the National Trust (03) 9654 4711 or the homestead on (03) 5981 2866.

For accommodation details, call Mornington Peninsula Tourism Forum on (03) 5987 3078.

'Women in racing' by Gina Perry

[This profile of a jockey was submitted to the *Sunday Herald* lifestyle supplement, along with profiles of a trainer and a bookmaker.]

When Prue Latchford was refused a jockey's apprenticeship because she was female, it didn't deter her. The year was 1977 and Prue was 18 years old. She could apply for a B Grade Licence (for riding in country races), the VRC told her, once she'd had more experience in amateur races.

Without the benefit of the training provided by an apprenticeship, she had to learn as much as she could about improving her riding from trainers and others willing to help her. She did a lot of trackwork and moved to NSW for three years, riding as far afield as Wagga and Gundagai where the opportunities to ride were greater and where she could afford to make some mistakes while she was learning.

At 23 she was granted her NSW licence, and in 1985, eight years after her original application, she returned to Victoria to ride the last of the barrier trials she needed and was granted a Victorian B Grade licence. It was, she admits, 'a real battle.' She found that things had changed while she'd been away. 'A couple of girls had been granted apprenticeships—that was a breakthrough, having women apprentice jockeys.'

Growing up, she'd already had plenty of experience competing against males as an only female. As a child, while her brother came onto the beach for a rest, she would sneak off with his surfboard and teach herself to surf.

At 16, she was one of only a couple of women surfing in the Victorian and Australian titles.

Today, at 31, Prue guesses that she is probably one of the oldest female professional jockeys in the state. She makes a 'reasonable living' these days, riding on average four or five times a week at country race meetings. She is one of eighteen female professional jockeys out of a total of 322. Behind her, the ranks of female riders are growing. Currently, approximately one-third of apprentice jockeys are female.

Still, she says, some clubs have trouble regarding women riders as anything but a flash in the pan. While facilities at clubs like Sale are outstanding, some clubs provide makeshift facilities for female riders, which, she says, are cramped, often isolated from the main buildings, and of a much lower standard than the facilities provided for male jockeys.

'I realise money is a big consideration, but that's a bit hard to believe when a club's trying to decide where to put a sauna for the boys when we haven't even got a shower.'

Despite this, female riders do well, she believes because, 'They tend to think themselves lucky to be able to do an apprenticeship so they tend to try harder.'

There is a sense of solidarity, rather than competition, amongst female riders. 'If a girl rides a winner, we're all very pleased—like it's a break for all female riders. We tend to keep an eye on the results to see how others of us are doing. We all try and help each other a lot,' she says.

She's seen a lot of changes for female jockeys in the past ten years. In the beginning, there were a lot of people who wouldn't dream of putting a female jockey on a horse. Nowadays, she says, while prejudice still exists, people are beginning to recognise that female riders have brought different techniques to their performance with the horse. The other striking thing she notices now, is the way female riders' view of themselves has changed.

'When I first started riding a lot of the girls felt that because they were in a male field they had to act like boys—and be rough and ready when they weren't on their horses. Today, most of the female jockeys take particular care to dress as females, act, walk, talk as females while they're not on the horses.

'When you're on a horse, you're not male, female, small,

old, young—you're all the one thing—you're all competitiors and you're all out there to do the same job.'

She would dearly love to ride in town, and her dream is to ride in the Melbourne Cup.

However, being a B Grade jockey who did not serve an apprenticeship, she cannot ride in town, a fact that she resents. 'I applied for an apprenticeship. It wasn't my fault I didn't get one, they just didn't grant them to girls at the time.'

While she's modest about her skill as a jockey, her determination is obvious, 'I'm certainly not a Michael Clark or a Harry White or a Darren Gauci, but I'm working on it.'

She sees herself as riding for as long as she is capable.

'While I've still got that killer instinct to win I'll keep going. I love being with the horses, and the excitement and exhiliration of the race. I think if I won Tattslotto I'd still want to be a jockey.'

'Prejudice ruins a dream' by Gina Perry

Sunday Herald, 4 November 1990

[This is the published version of the previous story. It appeared in the racing pages.]

When Prue Latchford was refused a jockey's apprenticeship because of her sex she was not deterred. The year was 1977 and Latchford was 18 years old. She could apply for a B Grade Licence (country races), the VRC told her, once she had had more experience in amateur races.

Without the benefit of an apprenticeship, she had to learn as much as she could about improving her riding from trainers and others willing to help her. She did a lot of trackwork and moved to NSW for three years, riding in such places as Wagga and Gundagai, where the opportunities to ride were greater and where she could afford to make some mistakes while learning.

At 23 she was granted her NSW licence, and in 1985, eight years after her original application, she returned to Victoria to ride the last of the barrier trials she needed and was granted a Victorian B Grade licence. It had been a real battle. And things had changed while she had been away.

'A couple of girls had been granted apprenticeships—that was a breakthrough, having women apprentice jockeys,' she says.

Latchford had plenty of experience competing against males as a child. When her brother came onto the beach for a rest, she would sneak off with his surfboard and taught herself to surf.

At 16, she was one of only a couple of women surfing in the Victorian and Australian titles.

Today, at 31, Latchford makes a reasonable living, riding on average four or five times a week at country race meetings. She is one of eighteen female professional jockeys out of a total of 322. The ranks of female riders are growing.

Currently, approximately one-third of apprentice jockeys are female.

Latchford has seen many changes for female jockeys in the past 10 years. In the beginning, few people would dream of putting a female jockey on a horse. Today although prejudice still exists, people are beginning to recognise that female riders have brought different techniques to their performance with the horse.

Latchford's dream? To ride in the Melbourne Cup.

However, being a B Grade jockey who did not serve an apprenticeship, she cannot ride in town, a fact that she resents.

'Under the sun in Kelly country' by Vin Maskell

The Australian, Observer column, 5 January 1998

For classic depictions of the Australian summer, you can't go past the songs of Paul Kelly, says Vin Maskell.

There are many great images of the Australian summer. Call them clichés or call them icons, they are images that have become part of the national consciousness.

Max Dupain's photographs of swimmers at Newport and Bondi beaches are etched in our memories, coming to life every time we go to the beach. The best known is his 1937 photograph, *Sunbaker*.

Russell Drysdale's 1948 painting *The Cricketers* depicts three thin men having a game in an outback setting, the lone fielder leaning against a verandah post.

Ray Lawler's *Summer of the Seventeenth Doll* became a turning point in local drama. Helen Garner's *Monkey Grip* exposed and explored love and addiction under the hot Melbourne sun.

Paul Kelly, recently inducted into the Australian Record Industry Association Hall Of Fame, has said that he mainly writes about love, sex and death. When you include summer within those topics you find a series of songs that are as important as the works of Dupain, Drysdale, Lawler, Garner and others.

Throughout his long solo career Kelly has sung about summer, telling stories about cricket, bushfires, ice-creams, Christmas, gaol, lust, parenthood, childhood sweethearts. Sometimes the season is a backdrop, sometimes it is the main image that propels the song.

Post, Kelly's first solo album (1985) included Standing On The Street Of Early Sorrows, a bitter-sweet memory of feelings for a childhood sweetheart during an Adelaide summer when it was always 35°C.

Reminiscence—and lost friendship—is also the theme of Under The Sun (1987). The narrator stands on a shoreline and remembers 'Leaving South Fremantle in a Falcon panel van/We were smoking Marlboro, always singing Barbara Ann . . . All day long under the sun.'

Melting, a 1995 song co-written with Monique Brumby, is a haunting story made powerful by the lack of detail. Kelly delivers his lyrics in spoken word, while Brumby's vocals remind one of Rickie Lee Jones. They recall family gatherings, melting ice-creams, youthful pranks, and, perhaps, arson. 'There was a hill/Black and smokey at the end of the day/We watched the fire trucks go back on down the road/ We heard them calling out our names /We were standing in the shadows/ Melting, melting.'

Kelly uses bushfire as a simile in Don't Stand So Close To The Window, a 1987 tune about an affair where 'the word on the wire/would be just like Ash Wednesday bushfire.'

Sex is cheap in pop music—but Kelly can sing about sex and give it some substance, some meaning or, at the least, some semblance of reality. Summer Rain, from the 1994 album *Wanted Man*, is a short, gentle, languid look at sex and yearning. Kelly's almost plain vocals are offset by some delicate piano and cello. 'She comes and goes like summer rain/I wait all day for summer rain/And when she comes I smile again.'

Blush describes a woman walking 'by the Indian Ocean', the breeze from the beach is playing with her cotton dress. Kelly mentally disrobes the object of his desire, wanting to taste the salt on her cheek and on her neck.

And Kelly loves his cricket. He pays tribute to The Don in Bradman, a long ballad he wrote in 1982, and jauntily sings the praises of David Gower in a ditty to the tune of Guantanamera. He also tells us where he'll be on Boxing Day in Behind the Bowler's Arm. (Ten rows back, Great Southern Stand.)

The Christmas period is a rich source of material. In

I Can't Believe We Were Married (1991), 'We danced in the kitchen on Boxing Day/I held you swinging in my arms to Marvin Gaye/Our Christmas ham turned green by New Year's Eve.'

In How To Make Gravy (1996) a prisoner writes to his family, regretting that he can't be home to make the gravy for the Christmas roast. Kelly has long been an admirer of US writer Raymond Carver and this song deserves to be regarded in that company. Poignant, heart-wrenching, but not cloyingly sentimental.

Perhaps Kelly's finest summer song—finest song for that matter—is Deeper Water, the title track to his 1995 album. The song begins and ends with a simple, classic image, father and child on the shoreline. In-between are five succinct verses about love, sex, birth and death. Musically, it features one of Kelly's trademarks—the quiet, scene-setting first verse and then the full band joining in as the story unfolds.

Kelly is not the only Australian songwriter to paint evocative summer images (try Sirens, by My Friend The Chocolate Cake, or Ocean Of You by The Black Eyed Susans, or Wedding Cake Island by Midnight Oil) but he has written more songs about summer than most.

Paul Kelly's summer songs are, of course, just part of his work. Land rights, human rights, addiction, cities, winter, and the darker side of love are among his other subjects. But the cover and booklet of his greatest hits collection *Songs From The South* (140,000 copies sold), shows a boy on a beach, holding a bat, the stumps broken. The sepia photos could be of Kelly. Or the boy could be a descendant of one of the figures in Russell Drysdale's painting *The Cricketers*. Or maybe he's a grandchild from one of Max Dupain's subjects.

Whoever he is, summer is calling him, singing to him, telling him about fires, and ice-creams, and love. And deeper water.

'Dog days' by Barry Garner

Age, 29 September 1997

It was early spring. The season of new beginnings. A time when you shake off the coat of lethargy that is winter and look forward to warmer times, happier times. The trees outside the Lost Dogs Home were beginning to sprout the leaves that would provide a backdrop of green for the concrete pens.

A young family arrived just after we opened. They wanted to adopt a puppy, so I led them to Block H, the adoption pens. The litter of kelpie-cross pups lay peacefully on their beds soaking up the warm morning sun. They came to life as they heard the children approach and tumbled playfully over each other trying to be first to get a pat. They seemed a nice family and, although I'm sure the children would have gladly taken home all four of the pups, their parents had given pet ownership a lot of thought and wanted to make sure the children made a sensible and practical choice.

I left them and went about my other duties, telling the family to take as long as they liked. After much deliberation, the family chose the female pup with speckles of white through her dark-brown coat. The pup bounded from child to child on her new red lead.

To see a young pup like that, heading off to a new home and a new beginning, seemed to fit well with the beginning of a new season.

Later that morning, I was out doing a round of ambulance jobs, which included picking up a fourteen-year-old dog from Pascoe Vale that was to be put to sleep. These jobs are always sad, but for some reason this one would prove sadder than most.

I arrived to find the elderly owner of the dog pottering around in the well-kept front garden. In hindsight, I don't think he was actually gardening, I think he was just trying to keep his mind busy and off the reason for my visit. Having seen me pull up, the man left the garden bed he had been staring into, walked slowly across the lawn and met me at the top of the driveway.

'Good morning. I'm here about your dog.' It is always difficult in these situations to know just what to say. The elderly man looked at me with eyes full of painful resolve. The decision to have his dog put down was weighing heavily on him. 'Come out the back and I'll show you where he is.' Nothing else was said. I walked behind him, down the drive to a double gate. We stopped at the driveway gate, and the man fumbled to open it as he called out, 'Come on, King.' As we entered the yard, the old dog rose slowly and tottered towards his master.

King was blind in one eye, his muzzle was grey with age and he seemed crippled with arthritis that nagged his hind legs. 'Come here, mate, that's a boy.'

The old dog's tail wagged slowly as he heard his master's voice. With the dog at his feet, the old man bent down, placed a shaking hand under King's muzzle and with the other lovingly stroked the dog's head. The old man started to tell me how long he'd had King, but his tears stopped his voice, and his sobs said he'd had him forever. I felt like an intruder, like someone eavesdropping on a very private conversation.

I began to look around the yard. Neat, well-cultivated garden beds bordered a perfectly clipped lawn. Young seedlings staked with thin pieces of wood were planted in perfectly straight rows. The old man saw me looking a the garden bed and stood up, wiping tears from his eyes. 'I love spring,' he said. 'If you come back in a month or so that bed will be covered in marigolds.'

I tried to picture it, a mass of orange flowers waving gently in a warm afternoon breeze. 'You know, I could work out here for hours and that old dog would just sit there and watch me.'

I could picture King and his master season after season,

planting, watching, waiting. They would have measured time only by the changing of the seasons. We walked slowly back towards the gate and up the driveway, with King waddling beside his master. Old King didn't struggle as I lifted him into the back of the van. I think he somehow knew what was happening. He just seemed to accept it like another changing season. The old man gently patted King as he lay in the back.

Again I felt awkward. I knew I had to be going, there were more jobs to be done. But how can you put a timetable on the emotion the old man was feeling? Tears rolled down his cheeks as he told me I could go. I put my hand on his shoulder and tried to assure him he'd done the right thing. The hard thing, but the right thing.

As I drove off in what was now blazing sunshine, I thought of the old man and his dog, and of how hard it is to say goodbye to old mates. I thought of the young children who had bought the kelpie-cross pup this morning and of the love that dog would give them as they changed and grew together through many seasons. Yes, it was spring time; changing seasons, changing emotions. Sometimes, in this job, all in the one day.

'Bourke to Collins: tales of the city' by Deborah Forster

Age, 11 April 1997

In Bourke Street it's windy. In Myer's window, chefs in tall hats are cooking pasta for the Salvation Army. A crowd gathers to watch and the sound of a woman singing high and sweet drifts out from the store. The chefs pour the pasta into colanders and steam climbs from the sinks.

Across the road an old man in a green cardigan and a flat cap takes a crumpled handkerchief out of his pocket, wipes his face, puts it back, stands with both hands in his pockets, alert, waiting. His wife and daughter have gone into Dunklings. They come out. The wife slips her arm through his. They leave. Children jump around. One shouts: Don't step on the cracks.

In Myer's food hall, the food is laid out for the crowds expected for lunch. Along the window fronting Little Bourke Street, people are lined up along the bench eating, drinking, looking out into the grey of the street. In the corner, I drink coffee. Two up from me, a woman wearing a white lawn bowls uniform, her hat pushed back a little, is eating something flaky, perhaps it's a croissant. Crumbs drift down to the paper bag. She has a cup of tea. Next to her, a man in a beige cardigan sips a milkshake. He says: It's a mild morning. She agrees.

That Mal Colston's a right one, he says. She agrees. I don't know, he says, everyone worries about everything but the important things. Mmm, she says. There is a physical gap between them, an arc, each leans almost into the person on the other side. He says: Unemployment, that's the thing they should be trying to fix, that's the thing that breaks their hearts. I spoke to a chap on the train. He's got no work, he's got children. Everything gets on top of him. At an age when the young should be enjoying themselves.

In the silence they look out into the street, the coffee

machine squirts and farts in the background, the occasional car passes.

From around here, are you? asks the bowler, stirring her tea. No, he says, I come from the country, though I lived here for nearly 40 years. She says: Country'd be nice.

We like it, he says.

Got children have you? He doesn't answer.

He says: We've come down for a show, going to see that Sunset Boulevard, you seen it?

The bowler says, Don't fancy it somehow. We'll see, he says, and tells her he's seen some good shows in his time, shows that when you came out of them you felt you'd spent your money well. And then he says again as if it rests on his mind, as if he's saying it to everyone sitting along the bench: Young people these days, no work for them, it's a tragedy. It really is.

It's time for me to leave. I put my notebook away. I was trying to write but their conversation drifted into my hand. The theatre of everyday is everywhere.

Upstairs, customers are a rare sight. A large woman is dusting things lightly, a small man in a suit, his hair clipped short, comes over to her and says: I'm going to tea now, is there anything you want? She says: Put the kettle on and I'll have half your bun. They smile. She looks sheepish. He looks at her fondly.

Grey lino leads to the Ladies' Lounge in Myer. In there, behind the parcel desk, the attendant chats to a shopper. Inside, there's a knitter, a woman on a mobile phone talking about weddings and a young woman eating hot chips while she watches a soapie on the telly. The white smell of vinegar laces the chips.

Down the road, in front of Katies, there is a demonstration about the wages Coles Myer pays to outworkers; a young woman has a microphone. About 30 people stand in a semi-circle around her. Across the road a spruiker with a microphone is explaining to people why they should eat at Hungry Jacks. He has a little speaker beside him, static crackles out. No one stands around him. Trams cut through the centre and drown out both sides. Further down, some people with a video camera are asking someone questions. They are all wearing black.

In Collins Street, it's spitting with rain. Three taxi drivers stand near their cabs. One is yelling, throwing his arms around, telling a tale with a raised voice. The others deliver him their respectful attention.

appendix two: Legal and ethical issues

Defamation and defence of defamation

What does it mean to defame someone? According to *The ABC All-Media Law Handbook* (Revised edition, ABC Books, Sydney 1997 p. 3):

> Defamation occurs when published material, identifying a person, conveys a meaning which tends to:
> - lower that person's reputation in the eyes of reasonable members of the community;
> - lead people to ridicule, avoid or despise that person; or
> - injure that person's reputation in business trade or profession.

Identifying defamation in a nutshell, Mark Pearson lists the following points in *The Journalist's Guide to Media Law* (Allen & Unwin, Sydney, 1997 p. 113):

- Defamation is a published statement which damages someone's reputation or holds them up to ridicule.
- It varies markedly between the States and Territories, with some relying mainly on the common law (case law) and others having their own defamation legislation.
- Journalists are more concerned with libel—the permanently published kind of defamation (as opposed to slander, the spoken or temporary kind).
- Defamation falls under both the criminal and civil law,

although most common is the civil where one party sues another to get financial compensation for damage caused to their reputation.
- Anyone responsible for the publication can be sued for defamation: including the journalist, sub-editor, editor, news director, producer, publisher and printer.
- Any living person or company can sue for defamation. This applies to most legal entities except governments.
- To establish a case, a plaintiff needs to show the material was published, it was defamatory (made others ridicule them or think less of them) and that they were identifiable (although not necessarily named).
- The defamatory meaning of a statement is known as an 'imputation'. The imputation comes from the words or images themselves as well as the total context of the publication.
- The imputation can come from the natural meaning of a word or from 'innuendos'—reading between the lines.
- The fact that you did not mean to defame someone is irrelevant. The court only looks at whether you intended to publish the material.

Pearson also points out that using fictitious names in articles can backfire:

> People who actually have those names can be defamed unintentionally.

Defending a defamation is quite complicated. *The ABC All-Media Law Handbook Book* says that

> it is lawful to publish defamatory material if you can rely on a recognised defence. These defences include speaking or writing the truth (usually on public matters), reporting what goes on in Parliament or the courts, or stating honestly held opinions.

Let's look at the above paragraph a little more. Proving the truth of a statement may not be as easy as it seems. The person who made the statement must prove its truth, and proving truth under laws of evidence is often difficult. The term *on public matters* is similar to the term 'in the public interest'. But what may interest the public (scandal about public figures) is not necessarily 'in the public interest'. It does not necessarily benefit the public. And stating *honestly held opinions* may be a defence, if you have evidence—facts—to back up your opinions.

Mark Pearson is associate professor of journalism at Bond University, Queensland, and author of Breaking into Journalism *(co-written with Jane Johnston) and* The Journalist's Guide to Media Law. *Here, he answers some common questions about defamation.*

Can a review be defamatory?

Yes, it certainly can. The defence against a defamatory review is that of fair comment. You must have facts upon which your comments are based. If you're reviewing a book or a CD you have the evidence to back up your opinion. It's best to use comparative terms, rather than extreme terms when reviewing.

Can I defame someone on-line, on the Internet?

Very much so. The Internet is just another form of publication. The complications are mainly to do with legal jurisdictions. It's such an instantaneous form of communication and the publisher (which could be the writer or the Internet Service Provider—that's a grey area) has little control of where the material goes. If material is picked up overseas it may break defamation laws of those countries.

Can dead people, or their estates, sue?

No, but be very careful not to defame the living in a story about the dead, particularly by associating the living with the questionable behaviour of the deceased.

Can I still publish something, even though I know it's defamatory?

This has been done many times, occasionally for ratings and circulation increase, but more often because the publisher has believed the defamation is necessary in the pursuit of some larger public cause. Of course, it's asking for trouble, so it would only ever be done after consultation with lawyers at the highest executive level of the organisation you work in. If a case eventuates, the courts will punish severely any publisher who has flaunted the law intentionally.

Will I ever become an expert on defamation law?

Probably not. It's a highly specialised, complex area of the law which changes every month, every day even. Even the top barristers and judges in this field have trouble keeping up with the developments and interpreting decisions. The most you, as a working journalist, can hope for is to be aware enough of the basics to know when to call for help.

Copyright

The Australian Copyright Council is a non-profit organisation based in Sydney. Its services include seminars, research, consultancies and free legal advice. It also publishes a host of information sheets, discussion papers and books. The Council (Information Sheet G13, Writers & Copyright) says that

> if you own copyright in a written work, you are the only person entitled to:
> - Reproduce the work: for example, by photocopying it, copying it by hand, reciting it onto an audio tape, or scanning it onto a computer disk;
> - Make the work public for the first time;
> - Recite or perform the work in public;
> - Broadcast the work;

- Transmit the work by cable to subscribers (eg on pay TV); and
- Make a translation, a dramatised version or a picturised version (eg cartoon) of the work.

Ideas and copyright

There is no copyright on ideas but copyright protects the way ideas, or information, is expressed. The Australian Copyright Council (Information sheet 34, Using quotes & extracts) gives three examples:

> The actual words, or order of words and paragraphs used in a newspaper article about the Olympics are protected but the information contained in the article is not protected.
>
> The information in a physics textbook is not protected by copyright, but the choice and combination of words used in the book are protected, as are any illustrations or charts.
>
> The idea of writing a biography of Miles Franklin is not protected by copyright, and nor is information about her life, but the manner in which the biographer described her life is protected.

Fair dealing and other people's copyright

'Fair dealing' makes it possible for writers of short non-fiction articles to quote other writers' works without having to seek permission. 'Fair dealing' means you may quote material for the purpose of criticism, review or reporting news. You must acknowledge your sources at all times.

The *Copyright Act 1968* (Cwlth), Section 41, states that

> A fair dealing with a literary, dramatic, musical or artistic work, or with an adaptation of a literary, dramatic or musical work, does not constitute an infringement of copyright in the work if it is for the purpose of criticism or review, whether of that work or of another work, and a sufficient acknowledgment of the work is made.

The Copyright Act, Section 42(1) states that

> A fair dealing . . . does not constitute an infringement of copyright in the work if it is for the purpose of, or is associated with, the reporting of news in a newspaper, magazine or similar periodical, and a sufficient acknowledgement of the work is made.

The Australian Copyright Council (Information sheet 34, Using quotes & extracts) says

> There is no standard percentage or proportion of a work or number of words that can be used without infringing copyright. In every case it is a question of whether an important, rather than a large, part of the work has been reproduced. Clearly, the number of words or proportion of a work which constitutes an important part will differ in every case.

Copyright and the Internet

What control do you have over your work if it is published on the Internet? Mark Pearson, in his book *The Journalist's Guide To Media Law* (p. 253), says that

> intellectual pirates copy other people's work at will, knowing there will be a minimal chance they will be caught. The only sure way of guaranteeing an author will be recompensed for the theft of their work on the Net is to only offer it on a pay-per-view basis, charging a fee which covers copyright.

The AJA code of ethics

The Australian Journalists' Association (AJA), is part of the Media, Entertainment and Arts Alliance (MEAA). Since 1993, the AJA has been working on a new code of ethics, one to replace the 1984 code of ethics (which, in turn was a revision of the first code drawn up in 1944).

Proposed AJA Code Of Ethics
(as published in winter 1998 issue of *The Alliance Media Magazine*)

Respect for truth and the public's right to information are fundamental principles of journalism. Journalists describe society to itself. They convey information, ideas and opinions. They search, disclose, record, question, entertain, comment and remember. They inform decisions and animate democracy. They give practical form to freedom of expression. They scrutinise power, but also exercise it and should be responsible and accountable.

Journalists commit themselves to honesty, fairness, independence and respect for the rights of others.

Journalists will educate themselves about ethics and apply the following standards:

1. Report and interpret honestly, striving for accuracy, fairness, and disclosure of all essential facts. Do not suppress relevant available facts or give distorting emphasis. Do your utmost to give a fair opportunity for reply.

2. Do not place unnecessary emphasis on personal characteristics including race, ethnicity, nationality, gender, age, sexual orientation, family relationships, religious beliefs or physical or intellectual disability.

3. Aim to attribute information to its source. Where a source seeks anonymity, do not agree without first considering the source's motives and any alternative attributable source. Where confidences are accepted, respect them in all circumstances.

4. Do not allow personal interest, or any belief, commitment, payment, gift or benefit to undermine your accuracy, fairness or independence.

5. Disclose conflicts of interest that affect, or could be seen to affect, the accuracy, fairness or independence

of your journalism. Do not improperly use a journalistic position for personal gain.

6. Do not allow advertising or other commecial considerations to undermine accuracy, fairness or independence.

7. Do your utmost to ensure disclosure of any direct or indirect payment made for interviews, pictures, information or stories.

8. Use fair, responsible and honest means to obtain material. Identify your self and your employer before obtaining an interview for publication or broadcast. Never exploit a person's vulnerability or ignorance of media practice.

9. Present pictures and sound which are true and accurate. Any manipulation likely to mislead should be disclosed.

10. Do not plagiarise.

11. Respect private grief and personal privacy. Journalists have the right to resist compulsion to intrude.

12. Do your utmost to achieve fair correction of errors.

Guidance Clause. Basic values often need interpretation and sometimes come into conflict. Ethical journalism requires conscientious decision-making in context. Only substantial advancement of the public interest or risk of substantial harm to people allows any standard to be overridden.

Index

A to Z lists, 58, 125
accuracy, 7–8, 9, 10, 64, 69–70, 81, 155
active voice, 98–100
advertisements, 35, 46
AJA code of ethics, 29, 194–6
anecdotes, 59–60
angle, 66, 73, 111, 118
anniversaries, 48
appearance, *see* interviewing, appearance for
appointments, 78
Arnold, Kate, 131
articles, *see* feature articles
as-told-to stories, 56–7
Australian Consolidated Press, 13
Australian Copyright Council, 192–4
Australian Journalists Association, *see* AJA code of ethics
Australian Writer's Marketplace, 35–6

background information, 77
balance, 10
beginnings, 124–30, 132–3
see also leads; precedes; titles

bias, 66, 89
The Big Issue, 37
bookshelves, 17
Bourke Street, Melbourne, 186–8
break-out boxes, *see* sidebars
Bright, Steve, 20–1, 38
brochures, 48
Buckell, Jim, 61, 144–5, 156

captions, 138
choice of words, 94–8
Clark, Mary Ryllis, 17–18, 72–3, 171–3
Collins Street, Melbourne, 186–8
comment pieces, 60
computers, 17
conciseness, 94–5
concrete words, 96–7
conferences, 47
contributors, 3
copyright, 26–9, 192–4
  permissions, 28
  see also Australian Copyright Council; rights
corporate publications, 2–3, 4, 38

crafting, 117–21
curiosity, 42, 85
Curtis, Maree, 10–11, 143

Daffey, Paul, 158–60
deadlines, 9, 10, 19, 21–2, 119, 164–5
defamation, 25–6, 189–92
desk, 18
directories, 35–6
see also telephone directories
dogs, 183–5
Doole, Rob, 161–3
drafting, 109–23
see also crafting
dumb questions, 83

e-mail, 17, 49–50
  interviewing by, 81, 88
eavesdropping, 68
editing, 110
  see also subediting
editorial opinion, 6
editors, 33–4, 124, 129, 141–51 *passim*, 157
endings, 130–4
essays, 5–6
ethics, 9, 29
events, 48
evidence, 69
experts as sources of information, 67, 73

facts, *see* accuracy
fair dealing, 193
fax, 17
feature articles, 4–6, 16, 42
  angle taken, 66, 73, 111, 118
  beginnings, 124–30, 132–3
  compared with hard news, 5
  endings, 130–4
  human element in, 6
  similarity to fiction writing, 6
  see also as-told-to stories; comment pieces; first-person articles; instructional articles; list articles; news features; profiles; promotional articles; reviews
feature writers, 6
  qualities needed by, 6–11
feedback, 118–20, 123
filing system, 17–18
first-person articles, 59–60
Forster, Deborah, 186–8
freelance writers, 3, 23–4
  business considerations, 23
  financial considerations, 22–3, 49
  see also marketplace

Garner, Barry, 183–5
goal setting, 19–21, 23
government authorities, 69
grammar, 98–103, 155
grave-digger, 79–80
Griffin, Michelle, 117–18
guidelines for contributors, 37
guitar-making, 158–63

Haddock, Kate, 27–8
hard news, 4–5, 65
Hawley, Janet, 85–6, 126
Hayes, Pat, 35, 128, 131, 135, 137–8
headlines, 125, 126–7, 128, 130, 155
health maintenance, 18–19

how-to articles, 57–8, 125
human element, 6

ideas, 42–53, 147–8, 193
  arising from research, 71–2
instructional articles, 57–8, 125
Internet, 17, 38, 48, 68, 194
interviewing, 8, 42, 65, 67, 71, 77–91, 130
  appearance for, 81
  appointments, 78
  equipment, 82–4 *passim*
  punctuality at, 82
  questions, 78–80, 83
  reluctance of interviewee in, 88–9
  transcribing, 86–7
  venues for, 80–1
  see also on-line interviewing; telephone interviewing
introductions, *see* leads
inverted pyramid, 5
Ivory, Dr Kimberley, 102–3

journalists, 3, 195

Kelly, Paul, 144–5, 180–2
Kiely, Michael, 13–15

leads, 125–6, 129, 130–1
legal considerations, 9, 155
  see also copyright; defamation
letters, *see* query letters
letters to the editor, 35, 46
libraries, 37, 47, 68, 71
linking, 112, 114–15
list articles, 58, 125
listening, 83

McCamish, Thornton, 26, 148–9

McCrae, Georgiana, 171–4
McGrath, John, 158–63
magazines, 4, 13–15, 36–8
  readership of, 1–2
  see also staff magazines
manuscript assessment, 120
Margaret Gee's Australian Media Guide, 35–6
marketplace, 33–41, 44, 49, 137
media directories, 35–6
multiselling, 151–2

Nankervis, Brian, 80–1
news, *see* hard news
news features, 59, 125
newspapers, 4, 48, 51
  readership of, 2
notes, 83, 109–10, 111
nouns, 97–8

observation, 67–8, 71
office, *see* work space
on-line interviewing, 81, 88
open mind, 69
openings, 124–30, 132–3
  see also leads; precedes; titles
opinion, 11
  see also editorial opinion

page layout, 155
pamphlets, 48
participating, 67–8, 72
passive voice, 98–100
payment, 152
  rates, 22–3
Pearson, Mark, 25, 189–92
periodicals, readership of, 2–3
permissions, 28
photographs, 34, 137–8
  see also captions

postscripts, 34, 136
precedes, 34, 125, 128, 129–30, 155
Press, Radio and TV Guide, 35–6
procrastination, 164–70
professional organisations, 69, 71
profiles, 54, 55–6, 79, 125, 129–30, 138
  see also travel profiles
promotional articles, 59
publication profiles, 39–40
publishing directories, 35–6
punctuality, 82

query letters, 141–6, 149–50, 152–3
questions, 78–80
quizzes, 34, 136–7
quotes, 113–15

radio, 47
readers' interests, 35, 44, 47, 48–9, 93–4
reading, 7, 11, 46
  in research, 67
redrafting, *see* crafting
rejections, 9, 141, 148–51
relevance, 10
Reporting in Australia, 88
research, 8, 64–76, 85, 124–5, 143
reviews, 60–2, 191
rhythm, 100–1
rights, 141, 151–2
  see also copyright

self-help groups, 69
series, 138, 158
showing and telling, 115–16
sidebars, 34, 134–6

specialist publications, 47
staff magazines, 45
staff writers, 3
straplines, *see* precedes
structure, 112–16
subediting, 155–6

tautologies, 96
telephone, 17
  directories, 69
  interviewing, 87–8
theme, *see* angle
titles, 125, 126–7, 130, 155
top ten articles, *see* list articles
transcribing, 86–7
travel profiles, 56, 135

universities, 69

verbs, 97–8
viewpoint, *see* angle

Walsh, Richard, 13–15
White, Merran, 50–1
White, Sally A., 88
Whitton, Rhonda, 23–4, 120
women jockeys, 70–1, 111, 175–9
wordage, 34
words, choice of, 94–8
  see also grammar; nouns; verbs
work space, 16–17, 19, 20–1
writers' groups, 119–21
writing, 43, 92–107
  equipment, 17–18
  health considerations, 18–19
  style, 3–4, 8, 38, 102, 115–16, 117, 156
  see also drafting; rhythm; structure